Shapes of
Philosophical History

FRANK E. MANUEL

1965
STANFORD UNIVERSITY PRESS
STANFORD   CALIFORNIA

The Harry Camp Lectures

The Harry Camp Memorial Fund
was established in 1959 to make possible
a continuing series of lectures
at Stanford University on topics
bearing on the dignity and worth
of the human individual.

To Ida and Leo Gershoy

Preface

IN TEACHING and in conversation with colleagues, I have for many years been exploring the central theme of these lectures. The Spring 1962 issue of *Daedalus* published some of my thoughts as work in progress. I was encouraged to develop these ideas further and to present them systematically when Stanford University invited me to deliver the Harry Camp Lectures in January of 1964. At the initiative of Gordon Wright, Executive Head of the History Department, the series was extended to the perfect number of seven.

I take this opportunity to thank the President, faculty, and students of the University for the warm reception accorded my wife and me during our stay on their campus. To complete my good fortune, the staff of the Center for Advanced Study in the Behavioral Sciences welcomed me as a Fellow returned.

With minor changes in diction and the expansion of an occasional reference, the printed version follows that of the public lectures. Crane Brinton, generous as always, read the proofs with his usual discernment. Brandeis University provided assistance in the preparation of the final text.

Not least among the joys of my lecturing at Stanford was the presence in the audience of the dear friends to whom this book is dedicated.

FRANK E. MANUEL

Boston, Massachusetts

Contents

I
The Wicked Dance in Circles:
Early Christians against the Pagans

THIS IS perhaps the appropriate moment to undertake a review of the shapes of philosophical history in the Western world, the moment when man's history as an earthling is about to end. I hasten to add that this is not intended to be a doomsday prophecy, but a statement of mere fact, for with the imminent exploration of other planets, the limits of our earthbound existence will be exceeded and transcended. When history becomes interplanetary and assumes a different quality, even we historians may have to recognize the reality of the change as we are catapulted from our provincial vantage point.

For the most part, however, these lectures will be looking backward rather than forward. Though the geographic dimensions of philosophical history were always, in principle at least, the whole globe, for the last two thousand years the discussions have largely been confined within the orbit of Europe, North Africa, and the Near East. Despite Voltaire's perverse initiation of his philosophical history with a few comments on the Chinese, chiefly to annoy sacred historians, the bulk of his reflections concerned European man alone. Herder never lived up to his pretensions to universality; Hegel did not linger very long among the "oriental despotisms"; and as late as the 1880's the aged Leopold von Ranke, writing a universal history, still restricted himself to the territorial limits of the ancient world. Whatever may be said in criticism about the derivative character of the works of Spengler and Toynbee, their final emancipation from the bonds of Europo-centrism is not among the least of their merits. From giving form to the history of a few Mediterranean nations, philosophical history has within our age been forced to encompass the earth, and soon may have to pass beyond it.

Similarly the chronological bounds of our subject have in theory been exploded at both ends—but again, only rather recently. In contrast to Greco-Roman reflections on the infinity of time, most Christian philosophies of history well into the eighteenth century counted a finite sum of about six or seven thousand years past, present, and future to be encompassed and explained. The full meaning of our new time-span covering billions of years has not yet penetrated our consciousness.

I

Let me begin by taking you back to a scene from Polybius, 146 years before Christ. This sophisticated historian, once delivered to Rome as a Greek hostage, had made his fortune there. By the side of the victorious hero Scipio he witnessed the burning of Carthage. (Appian recounts the incident from a part of the *Histories* that is now lost.) "Scipio, when he looked upon the city as it was utterly perishing and in the last throes of its complete destruction, is said to have shed tears and wept openly for his enemies. After being wrapped in thought for long, and realizing that all cities, nations, and authorities must, like men, meet their doom; that this happened to Ilium, once a prosperous city, to the empires of Assyria, Media, and Persia, the greatest of their time, and to Macedonia itself, the brilliance of which was so recent, either deliberately or the verses escaping him, he said:

> A day will come when sacred Troy shall perish,
> And Priam and his people shall be slain.

And when Polybius speaking with freedom to him, for he was

his teacher, asked him what he meant by the words, they say that without any attempt at concealment he named his own country, for which he feared when he reflected on the fate of all things human. Polybius actually heard him and recalls it in his history."[1]

Less than five hundred years later Scipio's dark presentiment came true. For three days eternal Rome was sacked by Alaric's Visigoths. St. Jerome, in the Holy Land when the news reached him, uttered a cry of anguish. "Who would ever have thought that Rome, this Rome which dominated every part of the world with its victories, would crumble; that it would at once be the mother and the tomb of its peoples. . . ."[2] Not so the Bishop of Hippo. Living in a seaport town some miles to the west of Carthage, near present-day Bône, Aurelius Augustinus, a Kabyle from Tagaste, contemplated the fall of Rome more philosophically, within the frame of a Christian world history, and then spent some thirteen years writing *The City of God against the Pagans.* The cyclical theory of history, which Polybius had once eloquently represented as a Stoic bulwark against the vicissitudes of fate and which now seemed bitterly appropriate for Romans, was rejected by Augustine with contempt. While they, the impious pagans, might go about in a circle, as the Psalmist had written,[3] the sound doctrine of the Christian lay in a straight line.[4] The world had had a beginning, and it was proceeding toward its appointed end.

If you will allow me to interpret the conceptions of Polybius and of Augustine broadly, very broadly perhaps, two archetypal shapes of philosophical history here confront each other.

[1] Polybius, *The Histories,* with an English translation by W. R. Paton, VI (London, 1927), 439 (a fragment from Appian's *Punica*).

[2] St. Jerome, *Commentariorum in Ezechielem Liber III,* preface, addressed to the virgin Eustochium, in Migne, *Patrologia Latina,* XXV, 75.

[3] Psalm XI, 9: "in circuitu impii ambulant."

[4] St. Augustine, *The City of God,* translated and edited by Marcus Dods (New York, 1948), I, 498–99 (Book XII, 13).

Augustine's *procursus* is by no means to be equated with the late eighteenth-century idea of progress, and I am aware of the spiritual chasm that separates him from Auguste Comte. Yet, there is enough of a relationship between them to initiate the intellectual chain here. Though Polybius is no Spengler, the cyclical theory too has a separate genealogy traceable from antiquity: once virtually unchallenged in the Greco-Roman world, partially submerged during the Middle Ages, rehabilitated with the Renaissance, and then proclaimed with prophetic pathos by Nietzsche and his followers, it is still a lively intellectual orientation in our times, even if it be anathema to the Russians and somewhat disloyal to the American way of life in its most recent dispensation.

Initially, for convenience and shorthand, I have designated these two modes of historical perception as the cyclical and the progressive: on the one hand the historical world seen as movement either to a fixed end, or to an indefinite end that defines itself in the course of the progression, history as novelty-creating and always variant; on the other hand circularity, eternal recurrence, return to the beginning of things, sheer reiteration or similar recapitulation. But do not take these definitions too literally. Since this is a historical inquiry, both concepts will identify themselves more completely in time. In fact, I should be loath to stop at any chosen historical period in the past 2000 years and say that here, in this particular thinker, the most perfect cyclical or progressive theory is incarnate. The ideas are fluid and I expect to keep them so. Even when men of successive generations repeat each other verbatim, their words have markedly different tonal qualities and connotations. There is a certain core of meaning that remains the same over the centuries, but only a certain core.

Like all great mythic constructions with a long history, the ideas of the cyclical and the progressive are Protean. When at intervals they are molded or fashioned by major philosophical minds, they assume specific shapes, but shapes that endure only for a historic moment. And if through time these two conceptions, clothed in a magnificent variety of vestments, like all nuclear ideas in our Western culture, have been forced to serve many strange gods in both Church and State, they also have managed to preserve a measure of autonomous existence.

The historical world-views known as philosophies of history are mirrors of the mind and sensibility of the ages in which they were composed, but most magical mirrors. Once an image is frozen upon them, men continue to see their portraits in that fixed image long after they themselves have changed. Thus the images come to enjoy a life of their own—not independent of reality to be sure, because there always comes a day when a new generation of men takes a fresh look—but in the strange world of the mirror which is the history of ideas.

If we follow these two shapes of philosophical history, the cyclical and the progressive, from the early centuries of the Christian era through the present, they will reveal themselves to be less a logical than a psychological polarity. In any period there may be a weightier commitment to one or the other, but neither has ever dominated the European intellectual field without the presence in some form of its rival. The shapes have been combined, subjected to syncretistic amalgamation, intermingled, then separated out again. Old patterns are never completely forgotten and from time to time they are taken out of the intellectual attic, refurbished, and restored. The yield is a rich fabric of historical metamorphoses.

These shapes of philosophical history are today still recognizable as competing intellectual and emotional alternatives, and we are continually choosing between them. Is man like Ixion in Hades tied to the perpetually revolving wheel,[5] or is

---

[5] Ovid, *Metamorphoses*, with an English translation by F. J. Miller (London, New York, 1916), I, 211 (Book IV, line 461): "There whirls Ixion on his wheel, both following himself and fleeing."

he Jacob dreaming of the ladder that reaches up to the heavens? And when we finally select an identity for historical man, whose role we are defining, in the most intimate psychological sense, but our own? The professional historian and the layman, the grand philosopher of history as well as the meek antiquarian scratching through his records, inevitably betray a preference for one of these opposing conceptions. Even when elements of both progression and cyclism are fused into some more intricate system, the historian never completely frees himself from at least a bias in one or the other direction.

Now nothing could be further from my intention than the marshaling of evidence for the purpose of forcing a conclusion to the conflict. Let me say from the outset that I shall not bestow the palm of victory upon one of the antagonists, nor do I mean to accept a facile synthesis of opposites. It is rather by illuminating the polarity, showing its multiplicity of forms and permutations through time, focusing upon crucial moments of the debate in Western culture, that I hope to establish the contestants as enduring alternatives of the human mind in its examination of historical experience, as authentic antinomes of historical judgment. These shapes are typologies by now profoundly imprinted upon our intellectual consciousness, and they do not rub off easily with argument either logical or empirical. The massive enlargement of the body of factual historical data over the last few centuries has not significantly altered the balance between the two outlooks. Evidence accumulated as high as the sky would not end the controversy. It is perhaps time that we stopped debating psycho-historical states of being as if they were contradictory propositions whose difference can be conjured away by another shovelful of fact or by the discovery of a fatal inconsistency in their formal exposition.

This much by way of introduction and a statement of the central theme that binds these lectures together.

II

The whole of the surviving corpus of literature inherited from antiquity testifies virtually without contradiction that cyclical theory possessed the Greco-Roman world. The intellectual and psychological atmosphere, pre-Socratic, Platonic, Aristotelian, Stoic, and Epicurean, was saturated with it. It affected the cosmologists, metaphysicians, political theorists, historians, poets, and even the superstitious dregs of the populace.

Among pre-Socratics like Heraclitus and Empedocles circularity is both a metaphysical and a cosmological principle. The fragment from the great Agrigentine poet preserved in Simplicius describing the course of the *Kyklos* still exudes a mysterious charm. "A double tale will I tell: at one time it grew to be one only from many, at another it divided again to be many from one. There is a double coming into being of mortal things and a double passing away.... And these things never cease from continual shifting, at one time all coming together, through Love, into one, at another each borne apart from the others through Strife."[6]

For later ages the dialogues of Plato have always been a rich and varied source of cyclical conceptions. In the *Timaeus*, an astronomical cycle, or "Great World-Year," is completed when the planets moving in different orbits and with different speeds finish their circles together.[7] Then a reversion of nature to the condition at the beginning of the great Platonic year takes place. Though the periodic destructions described in the *Timaeus* and the *Critias* were merely geological catastrophes like the sinking of the island Atlantis, or epidemic plagues, and did not entail the annihilation of the whole world, the survivors of these events on the morrow of the cataclysms are so

[6] G. S. Kirk and J. E. Raven, *The Presocratic Philosophers. A Critical History with a Selection of Texts* (Cambridge, England, 1957), pp. 326–27.
[7] *Timaeus*, translated by R. G. Bury, in *Plato*, with an English translation, VII (Cambridge, Mass., London, 1952), 82–83.

few in number and so terror-stricken that all arts and sciences have to be relearned from the beginning by small steps through a vast extent of time. Civilization itself thus becomes subject to a cyclical process. Plato's evocation of the intermittent cataclysms inspires horror: the emphasis is invariably on the destructive not the regenerative phase of the circular movement.

The cycle of political revolutions, to introduce an example from a different field of knowledge, was a fixture of Greek thought. Since even the ideal Republic of Plato must know corruption, the third book of the *Laws* presumes a historical past in which thousands upon thousands of political cycles, with states coming into being and perishing at intervals, have exhibited the same constitutions over and over again, from good to bad and from bad to good. Aristotle's study of the internal revolutions of the Greek city-states, which followed a probable if somewhat complex sequence of political forms, was by all odds the most influential exposition of the cyclical principle that was passed on from antiquity to the Renaissance. Polybius had adopted it as a complement to his circular theory of the rise and fall of states and empires. As he wrote in the *Histories*: "Such is the cycle of political revolution [*anakyklosis*], the course appointed by nature in which constitutions change, disappear, and finally return to the point from which they started."[8] The recurrence of events under similar conditions was never bemoaned as an evil by the ancient Greek historians. In fact only that which was able or likely to repeat itself was real. If history were not to be re-enacted in the same way under more or less equivalent circumstances throughout all future time, then it was a fleeting, trivial thing not worth writing about. This position, which had its classical utterance in Thucydides, remained the justification of the historian as late as Procopius.

[8] Polybius, *The Histories*, III (1923), 289.

Under the Roman Empire, which will be our primary concern for the rest of this lecture, the cyclical idea in a most radical form is commonly identified with Stoicism and harks back at least as far as Chrysippus, who was born in Cyprus of Oriental parentage and taught in Athens in the latter part of the third century B.C. A cyclical conception lies at the heart of his cosmology. Periodically the world is transmuted into fire, from which it had its birth, though the process is not necessarily catastrophic, but takes place rather gradually as a consequence of the slow exhaustion of the earthy and humid elements in nature. The final conflagration is a transfiguration, a divinization, an expression of the perpetual rhythm of life of the universal god Zeus. If later this cosmology without a Genesis was odious to the Christians, the translation of the theory into human terms was veritable anathema. The god of Chrysippus did not play about with innovations, but after each regeneration he reproduced exactly the same world with exactly the same creatures in exactly the same relationships. "It is not at all impossible," says Chrysippus in a dictum recorded by the Church Father Lactantius, "that after our death, after the passage of many periods of time, we shall be re-established in the precise form which we now have."[9] Another text of Chrysippus, quoted by Bishop Nemesius of Emesa, was even more circumstantial. "There will again be a Socrates, a Plato, and each man with the same friends and the same fellow-citizens, and this restoration will not take place once but many times; or rather, all things will be restored eternally."[10] Marcus Aurelius drew appropriately melancholy moral conclusions from this Stoic pan-cyclism in its Roman version. Meditating upon the "cyclical Regeneration of all things," he muses that "our children will see nothing fresh, just as our fathers too never

[9] Hans von Arnim, *Stoicorum veterum fragmenta,* II (Leipzig, 1903), 189 (No. 623).
[10] *Ibid.,* II, 190 (No. 625).

saw anything more than we. So that in a manner the man of forty years, if he have a grain of sense, in view of this sameness has seen all that has been and shall be."[11]

Since most of the leading Stoics were from the East, it is nowadays customary to trace their cyclical cosmology to Babylonian astronomical and astrological sources, when one does not drop back even further and identify the eternal return as a universal ingredient of mythic thought. Seneca specifically related his own version of the cycle of destruction and regeneration to Berossus priest of Belus, Hellenistic author of the *Chaldaika,* who is authority for the Babylonian belief that when the stars are united in the sign of Cancer a great conflagration follows and when they are concentrated in Capricorn a great deluge. The Roman moralist introduced pessimist anthropomorphic themes to explain the periodic cycle: the world was an arena of growing perversity until there occurred a revulsion in nature which first brought destruction and then a return to the original state of innocence. By Seneca's time the Stoic cycle had lost that air of emotional neutrality and even zest for new life which brightened Chrysippus' circular cosmology. In his *Naturales Quaestiones* Seneca's portrayal of the periodic annihilation is benumbing, like an Eastern apocalyptic vision.

III

In the course of their intellectual encounter with the Greek and Roman worlds, Philo, the major Judaic philosopher of the first century, and the early Fathers of the Church became aware of the grave dangers to a uniquely revealed historical religion that lurked in pagan cyclical theory.

Philo of Alexandria is always the figure to turn to for a foretaste of later Christian attitudes toward pagan philosophy.

[11] *The Communings with himself of Marcus Aurelius Antoninus, Emperor of Rome, together with his speeches and sayings,* a revised text and a translation into English by C. R. Haines (London, New York, 1916), pp. 293–94.

In his treatise *On the Eternity of the World* the Platonic ideas of periodic destruction were bitterly combated as "the worst of profanities," denying the divine attribute of beneficence.[12] As for the Stoics' great conflagration, he mockingly inquired why its proponents always insisted on a conversion into fire rather than into any other one of the four elements.

When limited to secular political history, however, and applied in a mild form, the circular theory was not always considered inimical to the Jewish faith. Philo accepted the doctrine of circular vicissitudes as an adequate description of the history of Gentile nations. Only in the end of the days, with the coming of the Messiah and the ingathering of all the exiled Jews, would the Law of Moses be definitively established among all the nations and the cycles terminate. Philo's reflections on the rise and fall of Gentile empires, "tossed up and down and kept in turmoil like ships at sea, subject now to prosperous, now to adverse winds," have led commentators to surmise that he was acquainted with Polybius. Far from condemning the cyclical view of history outright, Philo discovered here the operation not of fortune but of the divine Logos, which dances in a cycle, allowing each state its appointed turn at hegemony and thus bestowing upon the whole politico-historical universe the most perfect constitution, a democratic one—in his Aristotelian definition a form of government under which everyone had his opportunity to rule.[13] This coupling of an ordained unitary course under the leadership of the chosen people with a variety of prior cyclical experiences for those nations who were not

---

[12] *De Aeternitate Mundi*, in *Philo*, with an English translation by F. H. Colson and G. H. Whitaker, IX (Cambridge, Mass., London, 1941), 259.

[13] *Quod Deus Immutabilis Sit*, in *Philo*, III (London, New York, 1930), 95, 97. Professor Harry A. Wolfson, *Philo* (Cambridge, Mass., 1962), II, 420, translates this section as follows: "For cyclewise moves the revolution of that divine *Logos* which most people call fortune (τύχη). And then, as it continually flows on among cities and nations and countries, it allots what some have to others and what all have to all, changing the affairs of individuals only in point of time, in order that the whole world may, as one city, enjoy the best of polities, a democracy."

elected is a specimen of intellectual syncretism that we encounter not infrequently in the early Christian period.

Origen, a Greek Father born in Alexandria two centuries after Philo, in his polemic against the pagan Celsus had not yet broken completely with Platonic cyclism, and he even seems to have incorporated the idea of periodic purifications of the world through flood and fire. His dissent from the pagans was over the cause, not the history, of the cosmic disasters. They were not due to astronomical cycles and periodic conjunctions of the stars, but rather to "the excessive torrent of evil," which from time to time had to be purged by God.[14] If Origen's views with respect to the great cataclysms bordered on the heretical, he fully recognized the hazards of extreme and literal Stoic cyclism when adapted to the world of men. Such doctrine had to be condemned as a denial of individual responsibility and of moral judgment. "If this is admitted, I do not see how free will can be preserved, and how any praise and blame can be reasonable."[15] The pagans' defense—that they had never pretended Socrates himself would live again, but only someone indistinguishable from Socrates—Origen dismissed as a quibble.

Other Fathers of the Church—Justin Martyr, Eusebius, Gregory of Nyssa—were joined in mocking pagan ignorance of the beginning and the end of the world. If the repetition of things is infinite then the world is uncreated and God is at most a prime mover. Eternity knows no created time and therefore there can be no Last Judgment. But Christians believed that there was one Genesis, one Adam, and one set of Biblical begats and no other. Each event in the history of the two dispensations was unique and foreordained. Nothing was

---

[14] Origen, *Contra Celsum*, translated with introduction and notes by Henry Chadwick (Cambridge, England, 1953), p. 191.
[15] *Ibid.*, p. 238.

rehearsed. If the doctrine of Polybius were applied to Israel and to the Church, their sacred history would become subject to the same vicissitudes as all other states and empires—and this was preposterous. Should cyclism prevail, the singularity of the moment on Calvary and the pivotal events of Jewish history which had been progressing toward that climax would be stripped of all meaning.

The sacred generations, taught the Fathers, succeeded one another, every womb bearing novelty. There was a great beginning and thereafter ever new beginnings until the final end. If there was an apparent similarity between one set of historical events and a succeeding one, the former was to be understood as a prefiguration. Babylon prefigured Rome, David the Christ, the ark the Church. This idea of prefiguration, so crucial for Christian history, soon became a felicitous way of unconsciously assimilating the historical cyclism of pagan thought without injuring the truth of directed Christian movement.

The patristic rejection of Greek and Roman cyclism doubtless had many antecedents in post-exilic Judaism, and there are those who trace its origins even further back to Zoroastrianism. Be that as it may, from the age of the Apostles on, no Christian could believe in the new man of St. Paul who supersedes the old Adam and at the same time tolerate Stoic cyclical conceptions.

IV

In the first centuries of the Christian era both Judaism and Christianity went beyond mere reaction against the inherent evils of the cyclical theory. They invented a series of imaginative philosophies of history, all having in common a progression in temporal sequence, which could serve to replace the false doctrine of the pagans. In the sea of theological writings four philosophies can be distinguished, though they sometimes appeared in artful combination rather than singly: (1) a four-monarchies theory as interpreted from the Book of Daniel; (2) a triadic periodization derived from the rabbis and the Gospels; (3) a sabbatical millenarianism; and finally (4) an idea of secular progress, which enjoyed a brief vogue in the period between the Christianization of Rome and its destruction.

First to the Prophet Daniel. If one were to ask oneself what framework—not philosophy—of universal history prior to Hegel and Marx has had the most stubborn hold upon the Western imagination, has seen the most books produced within the confines of its grand design, one would have to admit that it was probably the visions described and interpreted in the Book of Daniel.

Since the Book of Daniel is not likely to be current reading in our generation, I should like to recall for you the second chapter and the seventh. You may remember that none of the Chaldeans could interpret the dream of Nebuchadnezzar, King of Babylon, because the king was resistant and therefore unwilling or unable to recapture it. Daniel alone performed a feat as yet unequaled by our contemporary dream-analysts. Not only did he offer a plausible interpretation of the dream, but he told the king what the dream, which had gone from him, was: a monstrous image with a head of gold, breast of silver, belly and thighs of brass, legs of iron, and feet of clay, an image that was pulverized when struck by an unhewn boulder which detached itself from a mountain. Daniel interpreted the four metals as a succession of four kingdoms beginning with Babylon. Unfortunately he was remiss and failed to name the other three, a fault which left both Jewish and Christian expositors through the ages completely free to select their own candidates from an imposing array of monarchies. The same theme was repeated in chapter seven in a vision of four beasts coming out of the river, which Daniel saw himself.

On its face the Book of Daniel purports to be the writing of a Jewish captive at the court of Nebuchadnezzar, whose reign is now placed in the sixth century before Christ. But since the first part of Daniel is written in Aramaic, the second in Hebrew, and many words have been determined to be of Hellenistic origin, a traditional unitary ascription is difficult to maintain. The orthodox Christian assumption that Daniel was written during the Babylonian captivity and foretold the coming of Christ was ridiculed as early as Porphyry, who in the twelfth book of his *Adversus Christianos* proposed the reign of Antiochus Epiphanes as an alternative date, a most commonsensical hypothesis coming from a pagan neo-Platonist. Today some scholars set the first chapters in the middle of the third century before Christ and relate them to common Oriental tales of a successful courtier dream-interpreter. The later chapters are generally attributed to a Palestinian Jew who flourished just before the desecration of the Temple in 167 B.C., and whose work is considered typical of prophetic visions composed to comfort the Jews under the Seleucid oppression, to assure them that the triumph of their persecutor would be shortlived and that a savior was at hand. If the final redaction of the Book of Daniel is a work of the Seleucid period, readers were probably supposed to recognize in the four monarchies Babylon, Media, Persia, and Macedon. But after Rome devoured Greece the last beast had to be Rome, and to make room for it later interpretations perforce dropped one of the intermediary elements in the series.

All this would be of interest only to Biblical scholars if early Western Christendom had not adopted the four-monarchies doctrine as its own. Justin and Jerome followed Judaic tradition on the Book of Daniel and thus gave it Scriptural sanction, though there may well have been an independent stream of influence supporting the doctrine from non-Judaic opponents of Hellenistic and Roman imperialism. The Fathers were primarily interested in interpreting Daniel as a crucial Old Testament prophecy of the coming of Christ, but beyond that they used the succession of the four monarchies to bestow a simple, comprehensive shape upon the bewildering histories of the Gentile nations great and small, by subsuming all of them under the big four.

The vision of Daniel transcribed in historical terms by Jews and Christians is not necessarily a progressive one in the sense that the rule of one empire is deemed superior or inferior to the next. The succession of hegemonies has a circular character since each one passes through phases of dominion and fall, but unlike the pagan cycles which are infinite in number the Danielic sequence is concrete and finite. Four monarchies—and only four—comprise the total real experience of mankind, and once they have run their course the final act of the historical drama must take place either in an eternal Messianic reign on earth (one Jewish version) or in the Second Coming of Christ and Judgment Day.

The correct identification of the four monarchies was no insignificant matter because it involved the core of Christian prophecy. If one rightly knew what the fourth monarchy was, then one would be able to foretell the end of the days and accurately read the other symbols both in Daniel and in the Book of Revelations, for prophetic language was supposed to preserve a consistent standard vocabulary. As the Danielic dreams and visions involved numbers symbolic of the passage of time, the expositors had rich materials on which to exercise their virtuosity. Once Western man is solidly rooted in an arithmetical formula, whatever it may be, he takes off, his genius soars and flourishes. In literally hundreds of works Bible commentators of all the European nations computed and recomputed the seventy weeks, the life-span of each of the horns of the beast, the duration of the cryptic "time, times, and half a time."

Among early Christian commentators on Daniel a certain provincialism often affected the designation of the four monarchies. When Orosius wrote in North Africa, Carthage was honored as one of the two intermediary monarchies and was coupled with Macedon in a logico-geographic pattern that encompassed the four cardinal points: Babylon and Rome, east and west; Macedon and Carthage, north and south.[16] After the collapse of the empire two ways were open to the commentators: either Rome was never recognized as fallen so that every succeeding hegemony was still Rome (the empire was merely translated to Byzantium), or some new wicked worldly power, whoever it might be—the terrible Turk or Napoleon—was assimilated to the fourth beast. Greek Orthodox writers had no difficulty in considering Byzantium the second Rome and applying details in Daniel to historical events in the reign of their most recent Emperor. Reformation historians normally considered Germany the heir to Rome and the four-monarchies doctrine marched on undisturbed in their universal histories. The dream of Nebuchadnezzar and the visions of Daniel proved themselves to be wondrously elastic. Each new age could be solaced in its time of tribulation with the belief that this was the last period of affliction before the Second Coming. The prophecy of the Babylonian captive stretched itself through the centuries, making room for new rulers by telescoping the empires of the past. The ten toes of the monstrous image could become ten geographic parts of the Roman Empire, or at a later date the ten barbarian tribes who split up its hegemony.

Perhaps the later commentators might be divided into "praeterists" and "futurists": those who believed that Daniel applied only to history before Christ and those who insisted that the

---

[16] Paul Orosius, *Adversus paganos historiarum libri septem* (Cologne, 1561), p. 38.

Book of Daniel contained within itself a record of all major events that were destined to transpire until the end of time, a total philosophy of history. Calvin, for example, was generally a praeterist, maintaining that the work was silent about the ages after Christ; but even he admitted that subsequent monarchies were at least prefigured.

Jewish interpreters of Daniel continued their expositions independently of the Christians, since the rabbis could never countenance Daniel as a herald of Christ. Instead they calculated the date of the coming of the true Messiah through a cabalistic interpretation of phrases and numbers in Daniel. Rabbi Isaac Abravanel at the end of the fifteenth century, following the opinion of Rabbi Ibn Ezra, identified the last monarchy as the Turkish. When his views reached the Christians in the early years of the Reformation they were widely attacked and his *Ma'ayne ha-Yeshu'ah* (*Founts of Salvation*, first published in 1551), translated into Latin by Buxtorf the Younger, became a focus of learned controversy.

Though there is probably no decade in European history since the invention of printing during which the four-monarchies doctrine has failed of a new interpretation, certain periods have been more prolific than others in this branch of literature. The Reformation and the Counter-Reformation enriched Danielic philosophical history, as Protestants and Catholics belabored each other over the appropriate interpretation of the horns of the beast. Those who fancy this kind of polemic can find hundreds of opinions set forth and either accepted or refuted in Andrew Willet's *Hexapla in Danielem*, published in 1610 with a dedication to King James I. It was Jean Bodin in France who, in his *Methodus*, leveled the first major attack on the four-monarchies doctrine as a historical schema, simply by pointing out that there had been many great hegemonies in the world and denying that the prophet had any summary intention of reducing world history to only four. The humanist reformer Melanchthon still subscribed to a traditional interpretation, ending up with the Roman Empire and squeezing the modern nations—the French, Spaniards, Germans, Saracens, and Turks—into the feet and toes of the image. John of Sleidan actually named his work on universal history, which was translated into many European languages and enjoyed wide repute, *De quatuor summis imperiis* (1558). When faith in the prophetic character of the vision faltered, the scaffolding was preserved if only because there was no other. In his introductory epistle Sleidan writes, "Now that way is most commodious which divides this world into four monarchies."[17] Once a shape has been imposed through the centuries it becomes difficult to cast off, even after it has lost its vitality. Revolutionary England with its Puritan millenarians was a fertile soil for the flowering of the four-monarchies doctrine and for prognostications of the Anti-Christ and the Second Coming. Joseph Mede's commentary of 1642 became authoritative. Acceptance of the Danielic schema was, however, by no means limited to the fanatics. Many among the greatest minds of the age composed works on Daniel: the poet and philosopher Henry More, the founder of classical scholarship Richard Bentley, Hugo Grotius, John Locke, and Isaac Newton. In the eighteenth century there was a falling off in Daniel studies and even the *philosophes* refrained from whipping dead horses. But in the next hundred years prophetic interpreters of the Second Advent tackled Daniel with renewed vigor, especially in the United States. There was an understandable flurry of apprehension on the American frontier when William Miller, finding incontrovertible historical proof in Daniel, fixed upon 1843 as the date of the world's end.

[17] Johann Philippson of Sleidan, *The Key of History. Or, A most methodicall abridgement of the four chiefe monarchies* (London, 1631).

v

An alternative Christian theory to Daniel in the early years of the Church was a triadic division of world history. Among the rabbis of the Talmud there had long been current a tripartite periodization: before the law, under the law, and in the times of the Messiah. When St. Paul adopted this formula he had only to substitute "under grace" for the third state. There are many examples to show that such triadic forms were not a mere manner of speaking, but were actually utilized in the writing of universal histories. In the twelfth century Otto of Freising's famous history established three periods: before grace, under grace, and in the time of grace after the present life. As late as Johann Carion's *Chronicle* (1532), a popular Protestant universal history for which Melanchthon wrote an introduction, the Jewish tripartite division was retained and the rabbis were quoted directly as authority.

Of greater moment in the history of the early Church than the broad triad was a sabbatical millenarianism, because the anxieties of Christian eschatology were deeply involved here, and the design, like so many shapes of philosophical history, was emotionally charged. Irenaeus of Lyons, a bishop of the second century, was one of the first to divide world history into seven millennia, the last of which would be the reign of Christ on earth. The idea assumed variant forms depending upon whether a millennium was conceived literally as a thousand calendar years or was a conventional term signifying an indefinite period of time, and upon whether the reign of Christ was interpreted materially or symbolically. The discrete intellectual elements of which this theory was constituted have been discovered in Iranian, Babylonian, and Judaic thought. Seven cosmic epochs, each of a thousand-years' duration, each dominated by the influence of one of the planets, was an astrological stereotype which the Hellenized Magi brought to Asia Minor. A literal exegesis of the Psalmist's wonderment that a thousand years are as one day in the eyes of the Lord facilitated the reading of Genesis as at once a description of creation as it had actually happened and a prefiguration of the seven-thousand-year history of the world.

Sabbatical millenarianism raised ominous questions. Was the seventh millennium, as Lactantius held, to be an earthly kingdom like the golden age of the poets under Saturn, or did the Last Judgment end the world at the close of the sixth? Justin's seventh millennium was still of this world, though it was characterized by a complete cessation of sexual activity. Would there be a new creation on the eighth day? Millenarian prophecy, much of it precise and meticulous, captivated the Fathers during the age of the Church when the Second Coming was awaited with great impatience.

By the late Empire, however, the expectations had become less intense and controversy over the nature of the future millennia of history gave way to a more worldly consideration of the historical role of Christianized Rome and its moral relationship to previous epochs. Eusebius wrote a eulogy of the Emperor Constantine, hailing the *pax Romana* which was now also *Christiana*. An air of optimism possessed the triumphant Church. St. Ambrose embraced the doctrine of progressive meliorism in this world. In a letter to the Emperor Valentinian he peremptorily brushed aside the pagan plea to preserve traditional Roman rites in the Senate. "Why should we do so?" he asked, "Has not everything made advances in the course of time to what is better?"[18] Though it has come late in the year of the world the Christian epoch is the abundant harvest, the vintage, the olive. In the same spirit the Christian poet Prudentius unfolded a historical design in which Rome's imposi-

18 St. Ambrose, *Epistola XVIII*, in Migne, *Patrologia Latina*, XVI, 1020.

tion of her imperial civilization upon the nations became a virtual precondition of the spread of the gospel: "Who would have listened in a barbarian world?" The protector of eternal Rome was now Christianity, not pagan ritual, and secure in her new station the City addressed the contemporary heathens in verse: "Let those who din into my ears once more the story of past disasters and ancient sorrows observe that in your time I suffer such things no longer. No barbarian foe shatters my bars with his spear, nor with strange arms and dress and hair goes roving through my captured city, carrying off my young men to bondage across the Alps."[19] The poet hailed the arrest of the Visigoths at the battle of Pollentia as a decisive Christian victory. Around the year 400 Christianity was moving precariously close to full identification with the earthly success and progress of the Empire.

But a mere seven years after the boast of Prudentius, Rome was invaded, atrocities were committed on Christian and pagan alike, and the aged Bishop of Hippo had to write his apology of God's way in the world to silence Christian murmurers who had begun to doubt and unbelievers who blamed the new religion for the fall of the city. In the presence of the awful reality of the collapse of Rome, historical consolations such as the Book of Daniel, sabbatical millenarianism, triadic periods, and Roman progress were rather feeble. Milk for babes perhaps. Christianity needed stronger meat. And this sustenance it found in the magnificent system of St. Augustine.

Though there were, as we have seen, all manner of historical theories from which to choose in the Christian world of the early fifth century, for most of his life Augustine had been rather neutral about them. He was more the passionate psychologist of religious life than the philosophical historian. Not

19 *Prudentius,* with an English translation by H. J. Thomson, II (Cambridge, Mass., London, 1953), 61.

that he ever underestimated the uses of history in pastoral teaching, particularly in catechizing the unlearned: the narration of events in chronological order from Genesis down to the contemporary Church could serve as an instrument of conversion, he wrote to Brother Deogratias, a deacon of Carthage, especially if one confined oneself to the cardinal points and avoided being dull. But the sack of Rome forced the problem of history from the periphery into the center of his religious life.

By the time his work was completed in 426, Augustine had established his myth of the two cities as the canonical philosophy of history for Western Christendom. To the elucidation of that vision and that of Augustine's medieval rival, the Abbot Joachim, and their fortunes through the ages, I shall turn in my next lecture.

2

Ascending Jacob's Ladder: The Way of St. Augustine or of the Abbot Joachim

I F I PLEAD what the Germans call *Narrenfreiheit*—a fool's license—and venture to survey the whole course of traditional Christian philosophy of history, I find that two prophets and a saint dominate the field without significant rivals. Of the three, the prophet Daniel provides the framework, the bony structure, particularly for secular history; Augustine, the orthodox spiritual doctrine, the moral and religious passion; and Joachim of Fiore, the heresy.

As we have seen, separation of the intent of the original Daniel from later commentators on Daniel is relatively simple. But it is not so easy to extricate Augustine and Joachim from the possessive grips of their followers. To rescue Joachim from Joachimism is almost as difficult as it is to free Machiavelli from Machiavellianism and Marx from Marxism. We historians have learned that in some hands influences have an erratic way of moving backward as well as forward chronologically, and we have to guard against visiting upon the fathers the sins of the sons.

Jacob's dream of a ladder reaching to the heavens is the image I have adopted for the Christian philosophy of history; but I hope to show that St. Augustine and the Abbot Joachim of Fiore had two different ways of realizing the ascent.

I

Once he had condemned pagan cyclism, St. Augustine was prepared to accept from his Christian predecessors without debate
certain formal shapes of history, because they were not his main
concern. There is something rather conventional and popular
about his sexpartite periodization of sacred history, with bench-
marks at Noah, Abraham, David, the Babylonian Captivity,
and Christ. The six epochs parallel the six ages of man and the
six days of creation. His flock apparently appreciated these
facile and orderly correspondences. For Gentile history, Augustine contented himself with a two-monarchies theory, the reigns
of Babylon and of Rome covering the whole time span. This
pattern allowed him to interpret every event in Babylonian
history as a prefiguration of Rome and in the end buttressed
his explicit condemnation of that prominent body of Christians
who had come to join the fortunes of Christianity with those of
the Empire. If Rome was really wicked Babylon in another
guise, then its iniquities had sealed its fate from the beginning.

Unlike the doctrine of the literal millenarians, Augustine's
six epochs are not of equivalent duration and he rejected with
vehemence the conception of a thousand-year reign of Christ
after Judgment Day. For Augustine the reign of Christ, the
last of the epochs, had already begun; and the eternal Sabbath
that was to follow the end of the sixth period was not of this
earth. His tolerance of millenarians stopped short of the more
presumptuous ones who interpreted Revelations to make specific prophecies of the precise year of the Second Coming. Such
foretellings were too much like those of the astrologers to
whom he had been addicted in his youth, before his conversion.
It is not ours to know this.

History was directional for Augustine in the sense that there was a relationship between true prophecy and fulfillment, but prophecy could never be understood by us poor mortals until after the fulfillment. Hence the vanity of the prognosticators. The movement of time appeared chaotic until one knew the goal. The Coming of Christ infused meaning into all previous history that was worthy of record in Sacred Writ. Though history had been laden with typologies of Christ, before He came there was no way of understanding that the event had been prefigured in Scriptures. Only the present could bestow full significance upon the past, an idea Augustine had already grappled with in a subtle passage of the *Confessions* on the relationship of past, present, and future time. The Coming of Christ had conclusively shown the coherence of one half of history; the Second Coming would reveal the providential design of the rest of history. Along with his predecessors, Augustine was prepared to admit in his Commentary on Psalm XXX that from Adam to his day a far greater portion of history had elapsed, had been acted through, than yet remained to be enacted. But the final moment remained veiled, and there is a stringent prohibition against probing too searchingly into the date of the end, an attitude similar to that of the rabbis. The end would come in the fullness of time. And as the centuries wore on the prophesiers were given the lie, while the Augustinian doctrine survived. The Bishop of Hippo had seen a vision far more glorious than the mechanical patterns of the millenarian periodizers—the Christian myth of the two cities.

II

The origin of the idea of the two cities has been traced to others —immediately to the Donatist heretic Tyconius, more remotely to the dualism of the Zoroastrians—but whatever the antecedents, it is everlastingly stamped with the seal of Augustine. While the rival structures of philosophical history current in his day became wobbly when the world managed to outlast the Doomsday commonly prognosticated by fifth-century Christians, Augustine's historico-philosophical conception of the City of God and the City of Man proved itself endlessly adaptable to new circumstances. One of those creative images in the history of mankind, it has served Christian historians for fifteen hundred years, and it still endures.

Allow me to recreate the Augustinian myth from the many poetic versions scattered through his works. Originally the City of God was designed as an angelic community to which innocent men like Adam before the fall would be admitted. But when a revolt took place in Heaven the cohorts of contumacious angels had to be cast into Hell, markedly thinning out the celestial ranks. In his turn Adam also sinned, and as a consequence his progeny for ever after were subject to the wily machinations of the wicked angels, become devils. The angels who remained faithful to God and whose numbers we know not are still in the angelic section of the heavenly division of the City of God; and the rebellious angels in Hell are part of the City of the Devil or the earthly city as it is usually called, lying in wait for their human opposite numbers on earth and occasionally participating in their evil-doing. Thus both cities transcend the boundaries of this world.

On earth the inhabitants of the two cities live so intermingled in body, though separated in will, that it is not always possible to distinguish between them.[1] Inextricably intertwined like two wrestlers, they have radically different natures. The characters of the two cities are a psychological study of opposites, finely drawn. "Accordingly two cities have been formed by two loves"[2] (*Fecerunt itaque civitates duas amores*

---

[1] St. Augustine, *De catechizandis rudibus liber unus,* translated, with an introduction and commentary, by Joseph P. Christopher (Washington, D.C., 1926), p. 81.
[2] St. Augustine, *The City of God,* II, 47 (Book XIV, 28).

duo): those motivated by love of self to the virtual exclusion
and contempt of God, and those by the love of God to the exclusion and contempt of self, those who live according to man,
and those who live according to God.[3] There are men of strife,
the *mali*, and men of peace, the *boni*. The men of the earthly
city enslaved by their concupiscence cannot see further than
their own desires and they lead turbulent lives in appeasement
of their lusts. The earthly city has its "good in this world, and
rejoices in it with such joy as such things can afford. But as this
is not a good which can discharge its devotees of all distresses,
this city is often divided against itself by litigations, wars,
quarrels, and such victories as are either life-destroying or
short-lived."[4] The men of the City of God, on the other hand,
even during their sojourn on earth, are already possessed by
the divine spirit of peace as they look beyond this world to
everlasting life in heaven.

The *procursus*, the history of men on earth, is a combat between these two invisible cities, each sustained by its aides in
Heaven or in Hell. On rare occasions it may become possible
for the antagonists to work together on temporary projects, to
coexist in this world, to act for peace in concert, but their underlying purposes always remain different. When men of the
earthly city seek peace it is only in order to be able to indulge
their appetites the more freely; for men of the heavenly city
love of peace is an emanation of their inner being, because even
in a just war the spectacle of cruelty and suffering saddens
them.

Augustine foretold the ultimate history of the two cities
with an easy simplicity that helps to explain his hold on the
Christian imagination. In this world, as it were in a sea, both
swim enclosed without distinction in the net until shore is

---

[3] *Ibid.*, II, 49 (Book XV, 1).
[4] *Ibid.*, II, 53 (Book XV, 4).

reached,[5] but after Judgment Day, when the men of the two cities will be separated out, "the pious people will be resurrected so that the remains of the old man will be changed into the new. The people of the impious, who from the beginning to the end were nothing but the old man, will also be resurrected, but only to be precipitated into a second death."[6] For the wicked of the earthly city, everlasting punishment in the company of the evil angels whom they join in Hell. For the just of the City of God, a final reunion with their soul mates, the faithful angels, whose depleted ranks are now restored to the full corps strength of the period prior to Lucifer's rebellion. Then a timeless Sabbath ensues. "After the resurrection, however, when the final general judgment has been made," wrote Augustine in the *Enchiridion*, "the boundaries will be laid out of two cities: one of Christ, the other of the devil; one of the good, the other of the bad; yet both made up of angels and of men."[7]

That Augustine conceived of his work on the City of God as a coherent, unitary world history we know from his own testimony in a letter to a priest first published in 1939. There he proposed a five-part division, of which the third, following a refutation of pagan doctrine, would be the origin of the City of God, the fourth its *procursus* or *excursus*, and the fifth its appointed end. A common English translation of *procursus* as progress, implying "movement toward the better" in an eighteenth-century sense, is now generally unacceptable. Augustine was as wroth with the worldly progressists among the Christians as he was with the pagan cyclists. True, the first part of

---

[5] *Ibid.*, II, 282 (Book XVIII, 49).

[6] St. Augustine, *De vera religione*, edited by Padre Domenico Bassi (Turin, 1941), Chapter XXVII, p. 231.

[7] St. Augustine, *Enchiridion de fide, spe et caritate*, translated by Bernard M. Peebles, in *The Fathers of the Church* (New York, 1947), IV, 463.

the book demonstrates that the life of this world, judged in terms of human suffering and sinful behavior, is no worse now than it was before Christ, hence no regression can be blamed on Christianity; but neither is there reason to believe that earthly things are definitely and lastingly better. Augustine was not falling into the trap that had swallowed Prudentius; he was not binding the history of the City of God to prosperity or the comforts of an imperial peace. With the Vandals approaching the gates of his own bishopric, there was no room for worldly optimism.

In a few places Augustine, wielding the instruments of apologetic, makes an attempt to find purpose in the barbarous behavior of the human monsters of the earthly city. Perhaps Alaric's Visigoths raped the pious virgins, he surmises, so that they might be saved from the deadly sin of pride later. But there is in Augustine always a strong agnostic element: he does not pretend to have fathomed all the secrets of God's design and he has no explanation for creatures like Nero and Caligula.

What, then, is the providential meaning of the *procursus* on earth, between Creation and Judgment Day? The answer lies in the history of the City of God, not in that of the earthly City. In Book XVIII the lives of kings may be synchronized chronologically with the pre-Christian saints, but the history of this abominable pagan world is a peripheral part of the work. The great light is always focused on the men of the City of God. The history of the Gentiles is merely tributary to the history of Israel and the Church; it has import only insofar as it affects them either as a scourge of God for sin or as an agent helping in the attainment of necessary ends among the chosen people. If there is an "ascendant trajectory" to the pilgrimage of man on earth, it is limited to the history of the City of God, and if there is a progression toward the better, it is a purely spiritual one.

The pedagogic analogy between the history of mankind and

the history of the individual does not in Augustine's writings normally refer to mankind as a whole or to mankind in the abstract, but only to the men of the City of God or to the Church as a mystical body. Whatever perfectibility there is in this world is the individual spiritual perfection of the elect of the City of God; there is no conception of the perfection of the species in its totality through time. Historical progression never refers to the progress of knowledge, which had no meaning for Augustine, and surely not to technological progress, for *machinamenta temporalia* really have no history.

History before the Crucifixion can be understood well enough in Augustine as a preparation for the gospel; but the question remains why it should continue after the decisive event has transpired. Augustine's solution made him the ecclesiastical philosopher of history for Christendom, as well as the creator of its second most sublime myth. The centuries after Christ constitute the history of the Church in a specific sense; and the delay of the Second Coming is determined by the time required for the recruitment of the Church. History will stop when the last in time of the saints of the universal Church shall have achieved his necessary spiritual growth on this earth; when "our full number may be completed even to the very last," Augustine wrote in his Commentary on Psalm XXXIV.[8] The decimation of the angelic chorus and its ultimate reconstitution thus account for the passage of earthly time. The predestined number of saints has to complete itself; the times have to be fulfilled.

Students of Augustine's works are aware of his profound ambivalence toward history and they differ sharply about the mood of his philosophical response to created time itself. On the one hand time has signified entry into sin and corruption, death and dissolution, the horror of history from which there

---

[8] *St. Augustine on the Psalms,* translated and annotated by Dame Scholastica Hebgin and Dame Felicitas Corrigan, II (Westminster, Md., and London, 1961), 217.

can be no emancipation until it ends and the just reach the harbor of permanent beatitude. On the other hand, time allows for the operation of grace and the birth and growth of the City of God. By itself temporal history is a narrative of miseries, and yet, viewed in the whole providential design, it conspires for the good, as willed by God for his creation—*etiam peccata*, even including sin.

III

If Daniel's succession of the four monarchies can be likened to a crude though sturdy amphora into which generation after generation poured its different concoctions until one fine day, sometime in the nineteenth century, it broke, the Augustinian vision has conquered time. *The City of God* can still be read without condescension by believers of all sects as well as by the infidels. But the Augustinian philosophy of history has undergone some baffling metamorphoses through the ages. When we turn to the followers and imitators of Augustine, the spectacle is rather drab. Though the outward structure of the two cities is reverentially preserved, the spirit has vanished and the conception has lost its original purpose and vigor. Those who live in the shadow of great form-imprinters like Augustine are condemned to the role of epigoni. The latter-day history of Augustinianism is as uninspiring as that of Marxism and Freudianism.

The first universal narrative written under Augustine's tutelage was that of the Spanish priest Paul Orosius. His *Seven Books of Histories against the Pagans* was meant to be a companion-piece to *The City of God* and it dealt primarily with the City of Man. In defense of Christianity Orosius makes the psychological argument that present horrors always appear more poignant than recollected ones, as he drones on with a chronicle of pagan disasters to prove his point. The providential design lumbers along creakily. The invasions bring the barbarians into contact with Christianity, so that our suffering may be the price of their salvation. The work of this loyal disciple, who wrote at Augustine's behest, is so frightfully tedious that it is hard to imagine why it was quoted so often in the Middle Ages or why a Renaissance Frenchman should have bothered to abstract and continue it, except of course for the reflected splendor of Augustine's name.[9]

In 1146 Otto of Freising wrote a *History of the Two Cities* in a conscious attempt to synthesize Augustine on the heavenly city with Orosius on the earthly city and to bring them up to date. A terrifying sense of the imminence of the end of the world and a deep feeling for the confusion of the times, the great strife within the Empire which he witnessed at close quarters, pervade this work, infusing it with a passionate quality that Orosius grievously lacked. While Bishop Otto went back to the framework of the four monarchies, he was faithful to the Augustinian idea of what he calls the *progressus* of the City of God, substituting this new term for *procursus* and thus drawing somewhat closer to a notion of progress. In his description of the history of each of the great monarchies, however, he committed himself to the cyclical pattern of an origin, a summit of power, and a fall into senility. Reflections on the impermanence of earthly things, on the mutability of historical events, even the imagery of the wheel, are frequent in his chronicling of secular history. Though the distinction is not yet complete, Otto of Freising is beginning to develop two separate historical shapes for each of the two cities, cyclism for profane history, meaningful progression for sacred history. Though Otto of Freising had no direct imitators, his *History*

---

[9] Jean de Courtecuisse (?), *Le premier* [*-secōd*] *volume de Oroze ... contenāt toutes choses dignes de mémoire ...* (Paris, 1526); formerly attributed to Claude de Seyssel.

of the Two Cities became a major vehicle for the transmission of the Augustinian historical world view, second only to the text of *The City of God* itself, which was copied and illuminated in the Middle Ages far more frequently than any other single work of a Church Father.

As we shall see, the Renaissance turned elsewhere for its historical models. But toward the end of the seventeenth century, the Augustinian theory of history was revived by Bossuet, then Bishop of Condom, in a grandiloquent *Discourse on Universal History*, which saw scores of editions well into recent times and became one of the most popular Catholic versions of philosophical history.[10] If Augustinianism was predestined to fall on evil days, none were blacker than those which saw this travesty put together by the great ecclesiastical trimmer of the age of Louis XIV. A court bishop, confessor to the King's mistresses, he introduced so mechanical an order into the providential plan that the bureaucracy of the French absolutist monarchy seems to have been its model. God's way in history is arranged like a set of Cartesian propositions; the mystery, the suffering, the cruelty, and the evil are drowned out by the sonorous bombast of the bishop who was so famous for his funeral orations. Bossuet wrote a secular history drama in the neoclassical manner, in which God appears at propitious moments to set matters aright. There are *coups de providence* as there are *coups de théâtre* on the stage. Whereas Augustine, confessing his ignorance, frequently drew the veil over the divine intent, the Bishop of Condom is far better informed, and he discovers the precise details of God's purpose in every historical nook and cranny. No doubts are permitted to remain in this sterile caricature of Augustinian providential history.

---

[10] Jacques Bénigne Bossuet, *Discours sur l'histoire universelle à Monseigneur le dauphin: pour expliquer la suite de la religion & les changemens des empires. Première partie depuis le commencement du monde jusqu'à l'empire de Charlemagne* (Paris, 1681).

Condign historical punishment was visited upon Bossuet for the composition of this insipid work. Since the *Discourse* had got no further than the reign of Charlemagne, some eighty years later an enterprising publisher commissioned the royal historiographer to write a sequel. The royal historiographer was Voltaire, and this was the origin of his *Essay on Manners*, a great manifesto of the eighteenth-century *philosophes* in the de-Christianization of history.

But this was only an episode. The French philosophers of the counter-revolution like de Bonald and de Maistre returned to Augustine, and in the twentieth-century world the revival of Augustinian philosophy of history has been the rock on which anti-modernist Protestant theology has built its edifice.

IV

If most modern interpreters are agreed that Augustine's City of God is an invisible community of the just which transcends the institution of the Church, by the twelfth century the visible directors of religious life had come to believe that the Eccelesia itself was the City of God on earth, patiently awaiting a day whose judgment could not but be favorable. To disturb this equanimity a new prophet arose in Christendom. Toward the end of the century Joachim, a Calabrian monk, who had known the mighty of this world at the Norman court of Sicily, a former Cistercian who had broken away to found a more stringent rule, was suddenly illuminated with a vision of the true meaning of the most cryptic passages in the Old and New Testaments, and was inspired to write of a new historical order in which the Church of Christ would be superseded by the reign of the Holy Ghost here on earth. With Joachim a great competitive conception of Christian history was born.

The Abbot Joachim, who had fled to the wild mountains of Fiore to write his prophecy, has to this day remained under

a cloud in the Catholic Church, even though during his lifetime he was honored by Popes and was personally never de-
clared a heretic. If Augustinian scholarship has of late assumed
mountainous proportions, Joachimite research has become
within the last fifty years a veritable Tower of Babel. There
are rival schools of thought on virtually every aspect of his life
and teachings. Some flatly pronounce him heretical; others
vouch for his essential Catholic orthodoxy, dismissing his fan-
tastic exaltation as mere hyperbole. He may be an example of
Greek Orthodox influence penetrating the West, since Calabria
was long in the Byzantine orbit; but then it is shown that Joachim attacked the Eastern Church. Parallels to his ideas among
twelfth-century German religious symbolists are hailed by one
faction among the learned and then deemed insignificant by
another. You can find the spirit of the Cathari alive in him, or
cite explicit condemnations of the Cathari in his writings; treat
him as a proto-Renaissance figure or stress the traditionalist
medieval character of his thought; identify him with his ex-
tremist Franciscan disciples or deplore their exaggeration of
his wilder side. Scholars have discovered in Joachim the hidden
inspiration of the whole of Dante's *Divine Comedy*, the clue
to the enigmatic Veltro; or they view the reception accorded
him in the *Paradiso*, where he appears by the side of Saint Bona-
ventura, as a judgment complimentary to the Franciscans but
nothing more. Finally there are those who have transformed
him into a great historical villain responsible for what they call
the secularized gnosis of all modern revolutionary movements.
Suum cuique.

Should we presume to rise above these parochial disputes,
Joachim appears heir to the exegetical, topological, allegori-
cal, and numerological traditions of the Church Fathers. These
he fashioned into a symbolism uniquely his own, which he
placed in the service of a new world history. The architectural

outline of his structure is simple, like a child's pile of blocks. There are three states (*status*) in historical progression, corresponding in their essential natures to the three persons of the Trinity. Each state is in turn divisible into seven periods (*aetates*) which are named after characters from sacred history. The *Concordance of the Old and the New Testaments,* the mystical key to the system and the name of one of his few authenticated works, is illustrated by a series of pairs.[11] Each saintly father in the first dispensation has an opposite number in the second; the saints of the third state, which is just dawning, are recorded only as precursors for the *Dux,* or Leader, of the new age; and Joachim regards himself as the equivalent of John the Baptist. The world is no longer an Augustinian struggle between two cities only one of which is capable of perfection, but a rising ladder of goodness and love. A commentary on Jacob's dream develops the symbol of the ladder with glorious imagery. In Joachim's writings the attributes of the second state which was drawing to a close in his day describe a Church unfulfilled. The reign of the Son that was born of the reign of the Father must give way to a new perfection in the reign of the Holy Ghost.

In one of its aspects Joachim's work was part of the perennially renewed medieval attack on the intrusion of secular lords into the control of the Church and on ecclesiastical worldliness. But on another level Joachim's was the most revolutionary attempt in medieval times to alter Catholic institutions. Joachim's gospel was neither Latin nor Greek, neither for the Pope nor the Emperor; it preached a new Order of Monks, not subordinate but dominant in the Christian world. Prophesying an era of the Holy Ghost and proclaiming the imminent establishment of the Kingdom of God on earth, he went far

---

[11] Joachim of Fiore, *Liber cōcordie Novi ac Veteris Testamenti, nunc primo impressus & in lucē editus* (Venice, 1519).

beyond the castigation of ecclesiastical vice. The existing Church, superior though it was to the carnal order of the Jews, was merely a transitional phase. Though I do not know from where the idea came, in Joachim's writings a cyclical conception has reared its pagan head again. The second state, the reign of Christ, in approaching its end has fallen upon evil days, even as the first had degenerated into the materiality of the Sadducees. And among the illuminated manuscripts discovered during the Second World War in Reggio Calabria, painted around 1200 as graphic illustrations of Joachim's visions, there is one that represents the three states as three interlocking and overlapping circular rings or hoops.[12]

To depict the persons of the Trinity as historical as well as theological realities, as Joachim did, was a most hazardous innovation when it entailed an order of progressive excellence among them, flagrantly diminishing the position of Christ and degrading the gospel to a prologue of an earthly state of perfection. Whether Joachim envisioned the total and absolute supersession of the clerical and sacramental Church or only its spiritualization, perhaps a shift of monasticism from a peripheral to a central position, remains moot. He never defaulted in his personal obedience to papal authority and he may not have been aware of the profundity of the chasm between his views and those of the institutions of the Church.

Doctrinally, the Joachimite prophecy was an open challenge to Augustinianism. In Joachim the reign of love on this earth, love from the heart, can dispense with the law of both Testaments; Judgment Day is indefinitely postponed and its awesome sting is removed by the transitional third stage of the Holy Ghost. The great expectation for which Joachim prepares the faithful is not an apocalyptic end of the world and a trans-

---

[12] Leone Tondelli et al., *Il libro delle figure dell'Abate Gioachino da Fiore,* 2d edition (Turin, 1953), II, Plate XI b.

cendent resolution in Heaven, but a far more immediate event, the appearance within a generation of the Holy Ghost on earth. As with the Greek Orthodox tradition of a benign apocalyptic Emperor whose reign precedes the Second Coming of Christ, so the third state of Joachim seems to ease the transition to the Last Judgment, rendering the break between this world and the next less frightful than it is in Augustinian Christianity.

Christian truth as it was taught by the Fathers and in the great medieval schools is no longer definitive truth to Joachim. Its inadequacy was rooted not in human frailty, but in the historical reality that the time of the final truth had not yet arrived. Joachim never spoke against the gospels themselves for they, too, were good in their day even as the laws of the Jews were in theirs, small comfort to the papal Church militant. One shies away from reading full-blooded nineteenth-century historical relativism into these provocative, if isolated, passages in Joachim's writings, but it is understandable why for centuries they attracted revolutionary millenarians both within the Church and outside it.

Joachim's numerological symbolism is an intrinsic part of his work; everywhere he finds meaning in the numbers twelve and seven and forty-two, and they serve to give arithmetic solidity to the equation of parallel periods and generations among the three states. The crucial date of the new era was 1260 years after Christ, proved with an exegetical virtuosity that ranges from Daniel and Revelations through Judith, who waited in her widowhood three years and six months or forty-two months which contain 1,260 days—ergo the reign of the New Testament will last 1,260 years. Such cabalism—*en passant* there are those who have found actual Jewish cabalistic influences from Spain in Joachim—is today rather alien to us. But Joachim's paradoxical combination of retarded modes of presentation with the most extravagant and bold new ideas is one that we shall meet with again among philosophical historians, peculiarly enough in two men from that same South Italian crossroads of Mediterranean culture, Tommaso Campanella and Giambattista Vico.

Joachim's cumbersome numerological apparatus was historically far less significant than the attributes with which he clothed his three states, above all the last one. Here the passionate longing for a new man breaks through, the man who has seen the vision of Jacob's Ladder and the heavens thrown open when the Holy Ghost descended on earth to teach him the fullness of knowledge and strengthen his will. "Life should be changed because the state of the world will be changed."[13] The active life immersed in dross must be replaced by the pure contemplation of spiritual man, who will also be wise, peaceful, and lovable, a man stripped of the vice of envious emulation. "We shall not be what we have been, but we shall begin to be other."[14] In the third state, after the spiritual renovation, each will be what he really is, full of pure and true love from the heart, not false.

The zeal that other mystics poured into their definition of God, Joachim devoted to the different characters of the three states. The *Concordia* tells us that in the first we were under the law, in the second we were under grace, and in the third we shall be under still richer grace. The first was knowledge, the second was the power of wisdom, the third will be the fullness of knowledge. The first was spent in the submission of slaves, the second in the obedience of sons, the third in freedom. The first in suffering, the second in action, the third in contemplation. The first in fear, the second in faith, the third

[13] Joachim of Fiore, *Concordia*, p. 21, column c.
[14] Joachim of Fiore, *Psalterium decem cordarum abbatis Joachim* (Venice, 1527), p. 260, column a.

in love. The first in starlight, the second at dawn, the third in broad daylight. Joachim's was a rich symbolic vocabulary that had resonances for centuries after his death.

v

In contrast to Augustinianism, the official Christian doctrine, Joachimism became a stream that flowed deep beneath the surface and only erupted at intervals. If you judge intellectual potency by counting books and references alone, the shadow cast by the Calabrian monk who bears the ambiguous title of prophet can hardly be compared with the towering Augustinian monolith. And yet, at fairly regular periods from the thirteenth century on, some follower of Joachim has been fired by the imagery of his progressionist history to preach of the new man of the Third Kingdom and of the eternal gospel. That Joachim was a hidden force in heterodox medieval thought seems proved beyond question by the inventory of his manuscripts—authentic, probable, possible, and false—that have survived in European libraries.[15] Many a thinker on the borderline of Catholic orthodoxy discovered in him a predecessor, and either adopted his writings or imputed his own to him, so that in time there emerged within the Church an amorphous body of Joachimite thought, an uncondemned heresy or one that was formally denounced only in its most extravagant pretensions. The uncompromising Franciscans of the generation after St. Francis, men like John of Parma, who looked upon themselves as the fulfillment of Joachimite prophecy and founders of the new Order, had to be repudiated as a threat to ecclesiastical institutions. For centuries, whenever there was an outburst against the papal Church, some element can be traced back to Joachim, whether it be among the Spiritual

15 Francesco Russo, *Bibliografia Gioachimita* (Florence, 1954), pp. 13–62.

Brethren, the Hussites, the Taborites, the Brothers and Sisters of the Free Spirit, the Anabaptists, or various millenarian movements of the fifteenth and sixteenth centuries. Printing furthered a recrudescence of interest in the Abbot's writings among the reformers: monks of the Augustinian Order arranged for the first publication of three of Joachim's works in Venice in the early sixteenth century, and, although I would not make much of the fact, Martin Luther was an Augustinian. Thomas Müntzer, of the more radical wing of the Reformation, defended Joachim from his maligners and pressed him to his bosom. "With me the witness of the Abbot Joachim is great," he wrote in 1523.[16]

For three centuries thereafter, Joachimite lightning kept striking in the most outlandish places. Rich Joachimite influences have been found in the writings of the great sixteenth-century French scholar Guillaume Postel, a heterodox Catholic who dreamed of a future world concord, though he seems to have been partial to a four- rather than a three-stage progression.[17] During the period of the Counter-Reformation there was born in Calabria another one of those feverish religious figures for which the area is famous, Tommaso Campanella. His worldly lot was not as fortunate as that of his medieval monastic predecessor. In 1599 he was imprisoned in Naples for raising a revolt to institute a sacerdotal utopia, the City of the Sun. With brief intervals of freedom he spent the rest of his life in ecclesiastical jails, his colossal energy crammed into a cell. He was subjected to torture. This was a man of many faces and I do not pretend to have solved the enigma of his personality: poet, philosopher of science, and defender of

---

[16] O. H. Brandt, *Thomas Müntzer, sein Leben und seine Schriften* (Jena, c. 1933), p. 132.
[17] William James Bouwsma, *Concordia mundi: The Career and Thought of Guillaume Postel* (Cambridge, Mass., 1957), pp. 56, 57, 76–78, 100, 276, and 285.

Galileo, Christian apologist against the Mohammedans. To some he has remained a great social prophet and I have seen his name carved among the heroes of the Revolution on an obelisk in Moscow's Red Square. To others he was a mystic, a believer in astrology, a *politique* who appealed with Machiavellian argument to the Spanish monarchy to defeat the Turk, assume world hegemony, and then subordinate itself to a new universal, spiritualized Papacy.

Joachim's language and the trinitarian symbolism of his historical frame are easily recognizable in Campanella's writings. In the beginning men were ruled by power, taught Campanella in his *Politica,* then followed the reign of wisdom, now the age of love is about to dawn. The City of the Sun will be the realm of love under a reformed Papacy. Like Joachim, Campanella spelled out the degenerative elements in each of the previous two ages: power turned to tyranny in the first; wisdom decayed into sophistical subtlety in the second.[18] Campanella does not dare repeat the names of the persons of the Trinity to designate his historical periods, but the fundamental Joachimite heresy, the spiritual happiness of the reign of love on earth, has reappeared.

Though the writings of Pietro Giannone in the eighteenth century were anti-ecclesiastical, the Joachimite theme and terminology were preserved, as the very title of his work, *Il Triregno,* testifies. Unlike Campanella's doctrine, Giannone's present Papal stage is a perversion of the first two, the primitive innocent dispensation of patriarchal Israel and the pure spiritual love of Apostolic Christianity, to which he would have mankind return in the final state. Giannone, long imprisoned for his opinions, was honored as a deist martyr among the

---

[18] Tommaso Campanella, *Realis philosophiae epilogisticae partes quatuor, hoc est De rerum natura, hominum moribus, politica (cui Civitas Solis iuncta est) & oeconomica* (Frankfort, 1623), pp. 369–70.

philosophes, but he really belongs with that strange band of south Italian dreamers of a triadic ascendant Christian world history culminating in the terrestrial happiness of a reign of love.

An even more famous secular evocation of Joachimism in the eighteenth century was Lessing's *Education of the Human Race,* where a progressive three-stage conception of history assumes a rationalist, freemasonic coloration. Lessing makes direct reference to the Joachimite mystics, and the three ages of mankind he outlined are virtual paraphrases of Joachim: the age of the Old Testament rule of external law through punishment in this world; of New Testament rule through future spiritual rewards; to be followed by the rule of reason and love internalized, which dispenses with external coercion. Wolfenbüttel, where Lessing was librarian, is among the known repositories of Joachimite manuscripts; direct transmission is therefore plausible.

By the nineteenth century the triadic historical formula is so commonplace that one need not look for specific Joachimite influence. But one branch of French romantic thought is consciously committed to his prophecy. Lessing's little work was early translated and published by Eugène Rodrigues when the Saint-Simonian cultists were in quest of a new theology. The reign of love on earth, the gospel of the golden age before us, are mainstays of Saint-Simonianism. Auguste Comte, a dissident Saint-Simonian, popularly remembered as the author of the law of the three states, proudly named Joachim among his predecessors in the *System of Positive Polity.*[19] George Sand was under Saint-Simonian influence during a crucial period of her life, and it was Ernest Renan, one of the first modern scholars to study Joachim's manuscripts, who drew attention

[19] Auguste Comte, *System of Positive Polity,* III, translated by E. S. Beesly et al. (London, 1876), 408–9.

to the affinity between the secret gospel of the monk in her symbolic novel *Spiridion* and the ideas of the Abbot Joachim.[20] As in all studies of influence, these intellectual chains have a way of trailing off into the absurd. By the end of the nineteenth century the stock figure of Joachim the prophet had begun to penetrate esoteric literature of the French *décadence*. In Huysmans's novel *Là-Bas* we find one of the characters expounding the mystic doctrine of the prophet. Foretelling the imminent reign of the Holy Ghost on earth he reasons in the inimitable French Cartesian manner: "Two of the Persons of the Trinity have shown themselves. As a matter of logic, the Third must appear."

I have tried to establish that the way of Augustine and the way of Joachim have been two enduring alternatives of the Christian idea of spiritual progression. While Augustinian pessimism about the uses of the City of Man has doubtless been the more constant Christian tradition, of late a kind of Joachimite faith in a new era of love here on earth has, astonishingly enough, found a sympathetic audience in the very See of Peter itself. But more of this in my final lecture.

[20] Ernest Renan, "Joachim de Flore et l'Evangile éternel," *Revue des deux mondes,* LXIV (1866), 142, fn. 1.

3
Ixion's Wheel:
The Renaissance Ponders the Vicissitudes

DURING THE Renaissance many provocative works were composed on the art of history writing, on the credibility of historical evidence, on the problem of biased judgment, but few that dealt principally with philosophical history. Though the period is alive with magnificent pragmatic and realistic histories, like those of Francesco Guicciardini, full of psychological wisdom, teaching discretion or audacity as the case may be, there is no single overpowering manifesto of the Renaissance philosophical position comparable either to the work in which patristic doctrine was enshrined or to the grandiose systems that began to make their appearance in the eighteenth century. Louis Le Roy's essay *Of the Interchangeable Course, or Variety of Things in the Whole World*, and portions of the *Methodus* and the *Republic* of Jean Bodin, are perhaps the only major exceptions.

Nevertheless, a Renaissance philosophy of history is readily identifiable, and by the late Renaissance it becomes remarkably rich in thematic variations. To illustrate this outlook I have convened a rather motley assemblage of writers from the sixteenth and seventeenth centuries, men from widely dispersed parts of Europe, different in character, and diverse in fortune. Two are the French humanists of the latter part of the sixteenth century whom I have just mentioned. Jean Bodin abandoned the religious life to become a jurisconsult, and at one time was high in the councils of the king. He was a *politique* in the wars of religion; but also a firm believer in astrology, demonology, and numerology. His *Republic* is one of the most influential works in the history of political thought. Louis Le Roy, a learned writer known as Regius, a translator of Aristotle and Plato, a royal librarian, suffered an eclipse until quite recently. To them is joined a third French humanist, La Popelinière, a Huguenot, more of a professional historian than the others, one of the first modern historians of historiography, a man renowned for his unique capacity to be objective while writing religious history in the midst of a civil war.

The Italians include two political theorists: the Florentine diplomat Machiavelli, the great *raté* who dominated one type of political thinking for centuries, and Giovanni Botero, in the service of the Republic of Venice, author of a treatise on *The Reason of State*. Two others are south Italian poets and philosophers of science, fixated men who led tragic lives in reckless conflict with their church: Campanella, whom we noticed in connection with the history of Joachimism, and Giordano Bruno, burned by the Inquisition in Rome in 1600. Of the Englishmen I shall discuss, Francis Bacon and Walter Raleigh were men of daring, curiosity, and misfortune. Fulke Greville, one of the lesser Elizabethan poets, has been introduced for his elegance, and the clergyman George Hakewill for his piety. Finally, to these I have added Giambattista Vico, who offhand seems out of place, since he died in 1744. He is a Janus-like figure, and in this context he will be read as a late Renaissance humanist rather than as the romantic philosopher of history whom Michelet re-created in the nineteenth century.

Aside from Vico, the lonely professor who lived obscurely and in poverty in the back streets of Naples, Renaissance philosophy of history was generally the profession of men of action who had rubbed elbows with the great and had watched the turn of fortune's wheel in the brilliant courts of Europe.

I

It is by now a commonplace that the rediscovery of the classical corpus during the Renaissance was accompanied by a revival of pagan cyclical conceptions of philosophical history. But this obvious fact must be circumscribed with a few caveats. So long as the European intellectual classes were Christian—that is, at least until the end of the seventeenth century—the Augustinian vision of the two cities moving toward their appointed and final ends remained profoundly embedded in their consciousness; and even when Christian faith faltered, there were powerful religious institutions which, especially in Catholic countries, enforced overt adherence. The circular world view, emerging from the shadows, never ventured to battle Augustine frontally, surely not with the same vigor with which he had once smitten the pagans. Cyclism reborn made its way surreptitiously, first insinuating itself into works on political theory, slowly carving out for itself a separate field, secular history, in which the circular views could be applied with relative impunity without disturbing the Judeo-Christian axis of world history. The idea of the City of God could not be challenged; but where the Gentiles were involved, a conception of the repetitive rise, apogee, and fall of empires as the way of the world could find support in Daniel skillfully interpreted and even in Augustine himself. Fuse the famous text from Ecclesiastes about nothing being new under the sun, the medieval *Ubi sunt* theme, and a historical interpretation of Daniel, and you produce a passable Christian version of Ixion's Wheel.

The crucial Renaissance revolution in philosophical history lies in the shift of focus from the City of God to the City of Man. Instead of the invisible City of God, where the *procursus* was of less significance than the beginning and the end, the substantial matter of the historical process now became the worldly state, the city, the commonwealth, and their palpable political fortunes, as it had been in the days of Aristotle and Polybius.

In probing the history of man on earth, the Renaissance theorists redefined the types of polity and drafted empirical laws governing the acceleration and deceleration of the historical cycle. In place of a unified Christian world history, there was now a sense of political and national multiplicity and diversity. Discovery of a pattern of similarities in the chaotic experience of states and empires throughout all time became a prime concern of both political theory and philosophical history.

History had become geographically as well as chronologically enlarged since classical times; and though there was still great concentration on the ancient peoples of Egypt, Babylon, Greece, and Rome, events from contemporary Christian political life could henceforth be included along with them in one philosophical schema. On occasion Western societies were even juxtaposed with examples from the infidel histories of Turkey, North Africa, and China. Since prudence dictated that the history of the Jews and the Christian Church be elevated to a separate plane, reasonable men were reluctant to meddle with them. The history of creation was ignored altogether, and the serious histories of the Gentiles were initiated with the Flood and the dispersion of the peoples after Babel, which served as a convenient great divide. Giambattista Vico continued this Renaissance subterfuge—if subterfuge it was—well into the eighteenth century. You look in vain for a significant mention of Jesus in the *New Science*. Despite a flirtation with the local Lucretians in his youth, Vico carefully refrained from relating the history of the Jews to the law of nations and the Jews were not made subject to the *ricorsi*. If this was caution, since the Inquisition still flourished in Naples in his day and he depended upon the patronage of cardinals and popes, it was also a traditional Renaissance form. On the continent one avoided intermingling sacred and profane history, for the sake of one's soul or one's body or both.

While it is impossible to measure the sincerity of religious commitments, many Renaissance humanists, apparently out of discretion, combined their cyclical theories with providential supervision. God had created the cycle and occasionally intervened to break it up. Louis Le Roy cunningly transformed the cyclical vicissitudes of empires into a Christian apology. God had deliberately fixed this order of alternating epochs of *heur* and *malheur*, "for men will soone waxe proud, and are easily puft up with prosperity and riches: and especially when they misconceave from whence such grace proceedeth, God is wont to send them adversities for their chastisment."[1] The Divine Schoolmaster had wisely introduced successive periods of virtue and vice in order to make vivid their contrariety. The pagan principle of discord, which lies at the heart of Le Roy's cyclical conception of the universe, was celebrated as an instrumentality of celestial governance. Bodin's *Methodus* carefully distinguished among the provinces of human, natural, and sacred history;[2] and when he expounded his cyclical theory he relied on Solomon's dictum for vindication and showed correspondences between human revolutions and those of the divinely ordered natural universe. La Popelinière's extraordinarily realistic *History of Histories* still treated Daniel respectfully as a historian who in a "prophetic spirit" had drawn up an account of the circular fortunes of monarchies with which the Church was destined to have converse. Through such simple accommodations the cyclical theory of history which Augustine had banished could be restored, provided, however, that one disavowed the eternity of the world and discredited the testimony of Greek traveler-historians who had reported Babylonian records going back hundreds of thousands of years. Once Louis Le Roy had delivered himself of a formal obeisance to

[1] Louis Le Roy, *Of the Interchangeable Course, or Variety of Things in the Whole World; and the concurrence of armes and learning, thorough the first and famousest Nations: from the beginning of Civility, and Memory of Man, to this Present* (London, 1594), p. 6 (verso); original French edition, Paris, 1577.
[2] Jean Bodin, *Methodus, ad Facilem Historiarum Cognitionem* (Paris, 1566), pp. 9 ff.

the certainty of Holy Scripture touching the creation of the world and the end of mankind, he could proceed with his history of vicissitudes between the beginning and the end without being molested.

II

The Renaissance writers were directly, almost slavishly, dependent on the cyclical theories that they found in the ancient texts. Louis Le Roy's translation of Aristotle's *Politics* is buttressed by a long discussion of the theory of revolutions, and decorated with parallel examples from Plato and Polybius and a host of other classical authors. He inaugurated his principal work on the vicissitudes with a summation of all circular cosmological theories inherited from the ancients; he regaled his readers with examples from Babylonian astrology, Greek mythography, Arab philosophy, as well as with the standard passages on the idea of recurrence from Heraclitus and Empedocles, Cicero and Seneca. In part this was a humanist display of erudition and did not necessarily imply respect for every ancient opinion cited. But the philosophical quintessence of the pagan views he adopted as his own universal principle. Machiavelli's major work was a commentary on Livy. Bodin, who controlled the whole body of historical literature, ancient and modern, as the extensive last chapter of the *Methodus* proved, swelled the more traditional classical documentation with references to Philo and the Church Fathers.[3] Perhaps one of the distinguishing features of the Renaissance revival of cyclical theory is the richness and variety of the historical material brought to bear on a thesis that in antiquity was limited to the experience of one or two societies.

Yet despite the new wealth of illustration, Rome remained the exemplar nation of the ancient world for Machiavelli, Raleigh, Bodin, and Le Roy, as it would still be for Montesquieu

---

[3] Bodin, *Methodus*, Chapter X, pp. 443–63: "De historicorum ordine & collectione. Universalis historiae scriptores."

and Toynbee. Here they all found the perfect historical cycle, an empire with a dated foundation, an apex, a long continuum, and a known demise. If Rome fell, what nation, however glorious it might now appear, could expect to live forever? Though the Venetian writers sometimes presumed that the Republic of Venice had broken the inexorable rule of the cycle, the Roman lesson endured as by far the most common moral refrain of the Renaissance historians and political theorists.

Though Aristotelian and Polybian political ideas are the basic substance of Renaissance cyclism, the conception had penetrated deeper and spread wider than historical consciousness alone: it had extended roots into astronomy and cosmology, into metaphysics, a sophisticated astrology, and a cabalistic numerology. Vasari suggested a cycle of artistic creativity among the painters whose lives he recounted that would later be adapted by Winckelmann to the history of art in antiquity; and Campanella in his *Politica* announced that "all religions and sects have their own circle," from belief in Divine Providence to atheism and back again.[4] The Elizabethan poet Fulke Greville charmingly expressed the cyclical political theme in *A Treatie of Warres*:

> Needfull it therefore is, and cleerely true,
> That all great Empires, Cities, Seats of Power,
> Must rise and fall, waxe old, and not renew,
> Some by disease, that from without devour,
>   Others even by disorders in them bred,
>   Seene onely, and discover'd in the dead.
>   . . .
> All which best root, and spring in new foundations,
> Of States, or Kingdomes; and againe in age,
> Or height of pride, and power feele declination,
> *Mortality is Changes proper stage:*
>   *States have degrees, as humane bodies have*
>   *Springs, Summer, Autumne, Winter and the grave.*[5]

---

[4] Tommaso Campanella, *Realis philosophiae epilogisticae partes quatuor*, p. 390.
[5] Fulke Greville, 1st baron Brooke, *Certaine learned and elegant workes of the Right Honorable Fulke, Lord Brooke. Written in his youth, and familiar exercise with Sir Philip Sidney* (London, 1633), pp. 77, 78.

A proper distinction must of course be established between a mere philosophical or poetic reflection on the mutability and transience of all things in either a Christian or a Lucretian spirit and a cyclical theory that is directly adaptable to history. To be sure the two sensibilities have a way of merging and interpenetrating. Raleigh's *History of the World* is a fair example of the domination of a narrative history by a tragic feeling of almost meaningless worldly change: "All that the hand of man can make, is either overturnd by the hand of man, or at length by standing and continuing consumed."[6] So Greville's sonnets on the vicissitudes of fate and Spenser's *Two Cantos of Mutabilitie* are remarkable poetic renderings of cyclical themes. But a theory of pointless vicissitudes as well as absolute historical Pyrrhonism—two attitudes that have had many partisans from the Renaissance down through our own day—cannot long detain us. The Renaissance expression of this view is doubtless more gracious, elegant and poetic, touched with melancholy. But at most it teaches moral lessons, Stoic or Epicurean, and its message is quickly exhausted for the philosophical historian.

When Renaissance writers dwell upon the unchanging character of basic human nature, so that the vicissitudes are merely a consequence of the interplay of human passions, mostly criminal, with fate, the historian's theory becomes a rather banal view of man in perpetual commotion. No concrete shape of philosophical history is discernible in this psychological jungle. Many expressions of La Popelinière approach such conceptions of the whirl, as do some of Montaigne's essays. La Popelinière wrote: "Each past event recurs. The motives and the occasions are the same. The faults and the imperfections of man neither grow nor are they diminished. They merely are renewed by a diversity of forms, the appearance of which makes the less astute believe that this renovation and fresh aspect is a change in

---

[6] Sir Walter Raleigh, *The History of the World*, 2 vols. (London, 1614), I, preface (unpaginated).

the matter and substance...."[7] Psychology has always been prone to devour historical theory, and vice versa. But those Renaissance writers who are committed to a specific form of historical cyclism have already divorced themselves from the black Shakespearean mood of a world full of sound and fury signifying nothing. Our main concern is with the thinkers who not only incorporated the cycle as a shape, but went on to illustrate its various stages with rich historical detail.

III

The work of Aristotle, the pagan *politique* to whom the Renaissance circular theorists attached themselves for main support, had been assimilated by the Church as early as the second half of the thirteenth century through the mediation of Thomas Aquinas himself. To the humanists observing the frequent internal revolutions of the Italian city-states and what, to their sense of tempo, were the bewilderingly rapid fluctuations in the external power relations of the great kingdoms, Aristotle became the ideal philosopher of the polity.

By far the most complex cycle theories of the Renaissance are derived from commentaries on his *Politics*, a work that dominated every discussion of the classificatory system of governmental types and of the dynamics of their repetitive sequence. A mere perusal of the scores of editions, glosses, and translations of Aristotle's text is quick proof that Renaissance political experience, viewed analytically and historically, was fortified by his theory of revolutions. Aristotle's work was always the point of departure, explicit or implied, and you established such innovations as you dared introduce by doing battle with the ancient protagonist. Jean Bodin's intricate descriptions of the *conversiones*—as he called the revolutions—of one type of gov-

7 Lancelot Voisin, sieur de La Popelinière, *L'histoire des histoires, avec l'idée de l'histoire accomplie* ... (Paris, 1599), *Premier livre de l'histoire acomplie* [sic], p. 39.

ernment into another, is a translation of Aristotle into the new language of sovereignty, an updating of his concepts, as well as a polemic against him.

Controversy over the most probable order of succession of the different forms of sovereignty within the state, the political-typological cycle, continued in the same manner well into the eighteenth century. Giambattista Vico's *New Science* is vibrant with so many novel psychological perceptions about the transformations of human nature that one tends to forget the more staid and traditional portions of his book, in particular a lengthy attack on Bodin's formula for the internal cycle of forms of sovereignty. In a dozen passages Vico is at great pains to show that his own thesis of the natural succession of governmental forms from the one (monarchy) to the many (aristocracy) to all (democracy) is consonant with Aristotle and in contradiction of Bodin. For Vico this three-stage cycle, which is repeated over and over throughout time, involves three different types of human nature, corresponding to the three levels of historical-psychological evolution through which all nations pass, an idea that transcends the mere day-to-day political revolutions of the city-state. Nevertheless Vico's abstract arithmetical presentation of the transformations—one, many, and all—is still within the frame of the Aristotelian typology. There are many mansions in the intellectual house of Giambattista Vico and in one of them he is, as I have said, the decadent Renaissance humanist absorbed with Aristotelian and Bodinian quarrels.

Parallel with the theory of the internal cycle of revolutions is another application of Renaissance cyclical theory, which is specifically Polybian in origin and is focused on the external power of the state, its birth, growth, flourishing, and decline in the comity of nations. The efficient causes of this cycle are described in terms that will be repeated again and again in philosophical history down to our own day.

The hubris of overextension became Montesquieu's explanation of the decline and fall of Rome, and has been entertained by men as remote from each other as John Adams and Arnold Toynbee; this fatal error was already a cornerstone of Jean Bodin's system in the sixteenth century. The height of the Roman cycle of grandeur and decay, as Bodin understood it, had been reached under the Republic, not the Empire; thus a moment of supreme civic virtue and not of territorial dominion had marked the zenith. It was the vast expansion of Rome that led to its downfall.

In at least one Renaissance theorist the efficient cause of the decline of power has a remarkably Malthusian flavor. Giovanni Botero's *Treatise concerning the causes of the magnificencie and greatnes of cities* is as materialist as one would expect from a servant of Venice. His argument on the future of cities, like his history of their founding, is based on "commodity." Cities decline because they fail to maintain pace with the growth in population. The food supply system of any agglomeration, even when it is aided by a commercial network, has its absolute limits, and when these bounds are reached, breakdown and disintegration follow. If the balance between the nutritive and the generative is disrupted—and this is normal experience in the "universal theater of the world"—people abandon the city that failed of its original purpose, to supply them with commodity.[8]

In those few passages of the *Discourses* where Machiavelli ventures to generalize about the cycle of power, he relates the loss of external dominion to the moral decay of the ruler, another idea that became one of the stereotypes of Western philosophical history. In the preface to the Second Book he examines "things pertaining to human life and human custom"

---

[8] Giovanni Botero, *A Treatise concerning the causes of the magnificencie and greatnes of cities,* translated by Robert Peterson (London, 1606), p. 91; original Italian edition, Venice, 1589.

in a Polybian spirit, concluding that "human affairs are ever
in a state of flux, they move upwards or downwards." Stages
in Machiavelli's cycle have moral attributes, expressed in terms
of his particular conception of virtue and valor, that are directly
related to the qualities of leadership. "Thus one sees a city or
a province that has been endowed with a sound political constitution by some eminent man, thanks to its founder's virtue for
a time go on steadily improving." But at a later date when the
city is on the decline and deteriorating there is nothing to es-
teem, for "all is besmirched with filth of every kind. And so
much the more are these vices detestable when they are the
more prevalent amongst those who sit on the judgment seat,
prescribe rules for others, and expect from them adoration."[9]
Later in the Renaissance, especially in the work of Louis Le
Roy, the inevitably corrupting influence of power, success, and
luxury is depicted with a richness of psychological insight that
is found in no previous philosophical historian, except perhaps
in Ssu-ma Ch'ien writing on the Han dynasty, or in the great
North African Ibn Khaldun describing the loss of fanatic soli-
darity (*'assabiya*) in the generations after a vigorous tribal
force has conquered a sedentary metropolis.

Louis Le Roy traced the pattern of growth and decay among
the great nations by delineating the different personality types
of the rulers at key sequential moments in the cycle. His was
a rather original conception: that each stage brought to the fore
its appropriate dominant character. "These great Lordships,"
he wrote, "were begun, and maintained by vertuous Princes,
accompanied with men at armes on horseback, and on foote;
hardened unto all labours, accustomed to watch, to endure hunger and thirst paciently, to drink water, being skilful and exer-
cised in armes." After the toughness and virtue which are the

[9] Niccolò Machiavelli, *The Discourses,* translated with an introduction and notes by Leslie J. Walker (New Haven, 1950), I, 354, 355.

marks of new beginnings, there followed softness and perversity during the decline. "So ended they under loose and voluptuous Lords; having their subjects depraved and corrupted by deliciousness proceeding of too much riches."[10] Again Louis Le Roy epitomized the psychological vicissitudes in a simple formula: "Such were the Authors or promotours of these Monarchies, alike in vertue and education: even as they also in whose raignes they ended, resembled one another in pleasure and pusilanimitie, and died wretchedly."[11]

This moral-psychological cycle of the nations drawn by both Machiavelli and Le Roy, which Toynbee has popularized in our day, is reproduced in Vico's *ricorso*. The first fathers of the theological state are robust and violent; the men of the heroic stage are cruel and punctilious; and during the breakdown of the last human age, men are slothful and oversophisticated, and what Vico calls the "barbarism of reflection" becomes the corruption of reason.[12] Then it is that a Divine Providence intervenes, in accordance with Vico's law of nations, to return men to a benign and simple primitive state and to initiate the cycle of civilization once again. In the same spirit Machiavelli had celebrated the appearance of a new man of *virtù*; the traditional Chinese court historians had saluted the rise of a simple peasant warrior who seized the throne; and Ibn Khaldun hailed a new tribe of Bedouin bound with passionate ties of blood to their desert leader. These vigorous types were all agents of renewal, emerging when an old circle of power had been completed.

Bodin taught that a state grows slowly until it reaches that condition in which its peculiar being, its mature essence, takes shape. Aristotle's biological conception of each being as des-

---

[10] Le Roy, *Of the Interchangeable Course*, p. 52 (verso).
[11] *Ibid.*, p. 53 (recto).
[12] Giambattista Vico, *The New Science*, translated from the third edition (1744) by T. G. Bergin and M. H. Fisch (Ithaca, N.Y., 1948), p. 381.

tined to fulfill its own nature is here adapted to the state conceived as an organic body. This perfection is of necessity finite and is known as the flourishing estate. Continuing the organic analogy, Bodin assumes that the peak of perfection cannot long endure. As for the decline of the state, its paths are as numerous and variable as individual fortune; there is no single ideal process of decay and death. While some great commonwealths fall of their own weight after having seized too much territory, there are many other causes of disintegration, such as civil strife and sudden epidemics. Bodin mixes the divine and the human, the wrath of God and military conquest by enemies. In his sixteenth-century world, declension was anything but gradual. Violent overthrow of a state's power, often at its height, appeared to be the normal destiny. Few polities that Bodin knew lived long enough to die of old age in the fullness of time, of what he calls an "inward sicknesse." The ordinary cycle, as he observed it, moved slowly until maturity and then rushed headlong into a catastrophic end, a reflection that bestows particular significance upon the study of the art of politics, whose aim is the preservation of the state, the protraction of its life as long as possible. Die it must, but death for Bodin is more tolerable if it "creepeth on" little by little, almost without being noticed.

For sharp contrast to this Renaissance temper let me juxtapose Hegel's contempt, very much in the German romantic vein, for those cultures which last long after they have reached the summit, after World-Spirit has abandoned them. Bodin's "long lingering disease" in the polity is still life, and if his political counsel can prolong its duration he has served the sovereign well.[13] When the end finally comes, the Stoic-Chris-

---

13 Jean Bodin, *The Six Bookes of a Commonweale,* translated by Richard Knolles (London, 1606), pp. 406, 408; the Fourth Book, Chapter I, is entitled: "Of the rising, encreasing, flourishing estate, declining, and ruine of Commonweales"; original edition, Paris, 1576.

tian calm contemplation of individual death is carried over to the state. There is no Spenglerian melodrama of destiny which destroys great nations and cultures, no Volneyian nostalgia over the ruins.

IV

But sensible as all this may sound, Jean Bodin and Louis Le Roy were also heirs to a great astrological tradition and contemporary witnesses of an astronomical revolution and the proliferation of a host of numerological theories. They were therefore understandably curious about the relationship between the cycle of nations and more measurable and objective scientific cycles in nature. During the Renaissance there were, of course, violent diatribes against astrology, such as those of Giovanni Pico della Mirandola and his nephew Gianfrancesco, who wrote an Augustinian treatise in 1519 dedicated to Leo X, demonstrating that Providence and sin were responsible for the calamities of the time and refuting all cyclical theories based upon eclipses, comets, and conjuncture of the planets, upper and lower, as well as the idea of fate, necessity, chance, fortune, and nemesis.[14] But the opponents of astrology were surely outnumbered by those writers who continued to seek the causes of the revolutions of empires in the movement of the spheres, as men had since the dawn of consciousness in the Middle East. Campanella sat closeted with the Pope, ambassadorial reports relate, performing ceremonies to ward off the influence of Saturn; court astrologers were common; and if the influence of climate on human nature was recognized by Hippocrates and Galen and admitted even by the most skeptical, why not the influence of the stars upon history? If the moon controlled the tides, why not the actions of men?

For all his learning and sophistication, Jean Bodin was a

[14] Giovanni Francesco Pico della Mirandola, *Liber de veris calamitatum causis nostrorum temporum ad Leonem X Pont. Max.* (Rome, 1519).

staunch believer in the power both of astronomic cycles and of chronological cycles to affect the destinies of states and empires. This was in no wise a derogation of Divine Providence. The cycles themselves were merely the orderly agencies of God —a crucial distinction that separated Bodin from the pagans, for whom chance and the fates and the movement of the celestial bodies were independent powers.

In the *Republic* of Bodin and in his *Methodus,* numbers are the major clue to the historical cycle. Not until Spengler will absolute time reckoning, sheer chronology, again play so significant a role in an important philosophical history. Bodin's numerology has a long tradition going back at least to the Pythagoreans and to Plato, and he was well acquainted with the cabalists; Spengler's number system is rooted in a morphological conception of rates of growth. Neither in Bodin nor in Spengler are we warranted in dismissing the numerology as mere aberration.

"Now indeed," writes Bodin, "there are but foure perfect numbers from one unto an hundred thousand, viz. 6, 28, 496, and 8128, amongst which the last cannot serve for the changing of Commonweales, for that it exceedeth the age of the world: neither the two first, for they are too little: so that but one of them can well be applied unto the chaunges of cities and Commonweales, viz. the number of 496, which is made of seventie septenaries of yeares, and a perfect number: it being also a thing by most auntient antiquitie observed, All cities in the revolution of five hundred yeares, to suffer either some great chaunge, or else some utter ruine."[15]

What the French Renaissance writers added to the Polybian reflections on the rise and fall of empires was a quest for scientific gauges that would predict the circular movement not only in its generality, but in its particularity. The inherited body of

[15] Bodin, *The Six Bookes of a Commonweale,* pp. 462–63.

respected astrological theory expanding from Ptolemy's *Tetra-biblos* had established a whole series of correspondences between the astronomical history of the heavens and events on earth. If Cardan was partial to the tail of the bear, Bodin refuted him and opted for eclipses. The respectworthy Jesuit astronomer Giovanni Battista Riccioli, compiler of a mid-seventeenth-century *Almagest*, who recorded all known past comets and eclipses, was careful to list alongside of them the catastrophic political events that accompanied them on earth. So realistic a historian of French social classes as Henri de Boulainvilliers as late as 1711 drew up a full-fledged theory in which the apogee of the sun and the location of the fixed stars, brought up to date with the newest computations of equinoctial recession by Flamsteed and the mathematical principles of Isaac Newton, were shown to determine world hegemonies, past and future, including that of Muscovy. Even in books in which descriptions of the cyclical movements of government are vivid with psychological insight and human empirical, rather than astrological, evidence, one should never be astounded by the intrusion of numerological theories.

In this field Bodin laid down an eminently scientific program of research for the future. The painstaking study of all past eclipses and their correlation with past political revolutions would lead to the discovery of the precise rules that governed the movement of the cycle. The correspondences are not yet known, he conceded, but they are not unknowable. And in this quest he is not a freak, only an illustrious example.

The desire to integrate the revolutions of empires with the new physical world system was a Renaissance passion that found an echo, as I have shown elsewhere,[16] even in Newton's strange revision of world chronology. These philosophical historians merely applied the method of physical science to a new

16 Frank E. Manuel, *Isaac Newton, Historian* (Cambridge, Mass., 1963).

field. That part of history which seemed most amenable to scientific treatment was chronology; since equal units of measurement were involved, it was reasonable for Bodin to expect that the time intervals between major events represented a scientific regularity whose key he had discovered. The cycle was punctuated by fixed chronological units.

The apparent contradictions between Bodin's astrological or numerological determinism and his faith in the uses of wise monarchical magistracy are conciliable. The stars determine, both Bodin and Le Roy are convinced, but in short terms they do not determine absolutely. As George Orwell might have put it: "All things are inevitable, but some are more inevitable than others." Astrology and numerology thus became parts of the politic art. Le Roy's description of the relationship between the necessary obedience of inferior to superior powers in an astrological sense and individual human free will is a paradigm for many similar theories of historical determinism in later centuries. "All humaine affaires do depend thereon, and yet are to be prevented by deeds: not that such effects doe necessarily come to passe, and inviolably by a fatall Law; but that they may be avoided by wisedome, or turned from us by divine praiers, or augmented or diminished, or moderated by nurture, custome, and instruction."[17]

Armed with astrological and numerological foreknowledge, Bodin's statesman might mitigate the influence of the stars or devise ways of assuaging their painful effects upon the body politic. Like a wise physician who can stave off death or at least relieve discomfort even in the most hopeless cases, the governor informed with scientific wisdom may postpone the ruin of his commonwealth. The *Six Bookes of a Commonweale* is a repository of sagacity directed toward the maintenance of stability in the face of overwhelming forces of corruption inherent

[17] Le Roy, *Of the Interchangeable Course*, p. 2 (recto).

in human desires, and even in defiance of the stars. But the degree of stability that can be achieved—even as the determinism —is always relative. The wheel grinds on, and the skill of the most astute sovereign can never stop its movement altogether; for in the end all commonwealths, even those which now appear to be in the bloom of health, must perish.

v

At this point the presentation of Renaissance commitment to circular theory requires emendation. It has perhaps become too pat. Are there no exceptions to this cyclical destiny? What about the visible triumphs of science and technology? Since it was early recognized that there were separate cycles of the arts and sciences, of public morality and of virtue, as well as of political power, what were the relationships among the various cycles? Did they revolve in harmony or were there contrarieties among the cycles themselves? What about those passages in Bodin, Le Roy, La Popelinière, Francis Bacon, Galileo, and Giordano Bruno, which hail the progressive scientific attainments of their age and mock those who blindly repeat ancient authorities? Bodin ridiculed the old men who could not conceive of new growth because they themselves were decaying. And even Machiavelli in a passage of profound self-revelation half jestingly derided his own excessive adulation of the ancients. Before we conclude, then, we are forced to open the question of the conception of secular progress in the late Renaissance and its relation to cyclical theory.

The quarrel of the ancients and the moderns, long recognized as one of the seedbeds of the idea of progress, has usually been studied in its literary phase in France and England during the late seventeenth century. Actually, many of the central issues had already been argued by Italian literary critics in the sixteenth century; and if one extends the problem beyond the confines of the aesthetic, it is soon apparent that the "quarrel" has been an enduring one in European intellectual history, with roots in the Church Fathers, a revival in the Middle Ages, and a flowering in the Renaissance, and that it has lived on into our own time. A critical estimate of Greek and Roman creative genius has always been a clue to the historical world view of a later age; but the evidence of this intellectual test must be interpreted with care and a decent respect for the complexity of the materials.

On its face the idea of Renaissance, or rebirth, implies a cycle and a low valuation of the immediately antecedent world, the medieval, the one in the middle between the ancients and the moderns. But the revival of learning led in some quarters to so great an exaltation of classical literary geniuses and philosophers, that an impression of contemporary inferiority to the ancients is inescapable. Viewed against this background, many of the cyclical theories of the Renaissance, strange as it may seem, were directed not against the idea of progress, for it had not yet come into existence in its modern guise, but against the concept of regression, of an absolute and irreversible fall from the pinnacle of excellence of the ancients, who had become final and definitive models of artistic and literary forms. In contradiction of the blind worship of the past, the cyclical historical theorist says that all things move in a circle and therefore our turn too has come, after the fallow period of the Middle Ages, to be as great as the ancients. We are, to be sure, not likely to maintain our superiority any longer than they did, but we can surely equal them. Thus a circular theory became optimist by implication.

Sometimes the same cyclical writers went even a step further. There are individual respects in which we have outstripped the ancients, such as science, philosophy, religion, or technology. Here examples are proffered that will be repeated *ad nauseam* for centuries: modern advances in firearms and military engines, the printing press and the compass, medical discoveries. A mammoth compendium of these instances of modern superiority over the ancients was collected by the English clergyman George Hakewill in *An apologie or declaration of the power and providence of God in the government of the world. Consisting in an examination and censure of the common errour touching natures perpetuall and universall decay* (1627). If an Italian literary critic of the sixteenth century cannot prove that the moderns have produced a greater epic poem than Homer, or even that they have equaled the Greek tragedians, he can still show that the moderns have invented new literary genres such as tragicomedy for which no prototypes existed in the ancient world. And humanists like Giovanni Francesco Pico della Mirandola can hold that the Christian philosophers Augustine, Thomas, Albertus Magnus, Duns Scotus, and Savonarola have been superior to the pagans in religion and morality: there are passages in the *Two Books on the Study of Divine and Human Philosophy* where the philosophical chain from Socrates onward is depicted as a fairly unbroken series of gradations upward in excellence, though only persons capable of appreciating and learning from the wisdom of their predecessors are included.[18]

When the literary quarrel in late seventeenth-century France moves onto the center of the stage, many of the Renaissance arguments are reiterated and refined—in our view often to the point of absurdity. In each of the genres the merits of the ancients and the moderns are compared in detail and the latter are revealed to have some excellences that the former do not possess. The decision of Charles Perrault is for the moderns, who have the advantage of time and can choose prototypes

---

[18] Giovanni Francesco Pico della Mirandola, *De rerum praenotione libri novem ... De studio divinae & humanae philosophiae: Duo* (Strasbourg, 1507), Book I, Chapter VII (unpaginated).

from a greater array of models. Moderns can learn from many more sources than could ancients, and though nature is no more prolific in genius among men in one generation than in its predecessor, sheer accumulation of examples itself becomes an advantage.

But none of these theories dealing with specific modern "proficiencies" in technology, philosophy, or literature remotely approach the nineteenth-century idea of progress. They lack at least three essential attributes of the later doctrine: universal inclusiveness, inevitability, and infinity. The moderns of the late Renaissance quarrel are usually on the defensive, merely staking out for themselves restricted areas of uncontested excellence. Francis Bacon's inventory of the state of knowledge was just that sort of stock-taking; science appeared to be one of the fields of accumulative knowledge. His famous dictum in *The Advancement of Learning*—"And to speak truly, 'Antiquitas saeculi juventus mundi.' These times are the ancient times, when the world is ancient, and not those which we account ancient *ordine retrogrado,* by a computation backward from ourselves"—was never generalized to all things.[19] In morals the wheel was still cyclical and Bacon's contemporaries, with their absorption in vice and luxury, in his judgment were "somewhat upon the descent of the wheel."[20] La Popelinière, after enumerating the modern augmentations, the discoveries on land and sea, and the many technological achievements, sardonically added the growth of effeminacy and the spread of disease.[21] Pascal carefully distinguished between scientific progression and moral progression.

Bruno preserved the image of Ixion's Wheel when depicting

19 Francis Bacon, *The Advancement of Learning* (1605) (Oxford, 1951), p. 38; a similar formula had already been used by Giordano Bruno in 1584: "voglio dire che noi siamo piú vecchi et abbiamo piú lunga età che i nostri predecessori." *La Cena de le Ceneri,* edited by Giovanni Aquilecchia (Milan, 1955), pp. 104–5.
20 Bacon, *The Advancement of Learning,* p. 136.
21 Lancelot Voisin, sieur de La Popelinière, *Les Trois mondes* (Paris, 1582), Book III, p. 51.

the moral destiny of man in his dialogue *Of Heroic Enthusiasms*;[22] and his famous circumstantial presentation of the continuous achievements of astronomy from the time of the ancient Greeks down, in *The Ash Wednesday Supper*, was less in the service of an abstract idea of progress than an apology and justification for science itself, against his hated enemies, the pedantic grammarians.[23] Le Roy's equation of the cyclical rhythms of military power and of the arts and sciences is a sport from cyclical theories of the Renaissance. Usually the rhythms of power and learning are thought of as contrary.

Thus the paradoxical arguments of Rousseau's *Discourse on the Arts and Sciences* were a long time in preparation. In fact, through most of the eighteenth century the idea of progression involved the notion of superiority over the ancients only in certain respects, and at the cost of a compensatory loss in others. Such stars in the galaxy of progressivist theory as Turgot, Mme. de Staël, and even Saint-Simon at one period of his life, foresaw an impoverishment of the imagination as the price of scientific advance. Total progress in all realms of being—the full-blown theory—is a late eighteenth-, really a nineteenth-century French concept, as we shall see.

In summary, Renaissance cyclical theory may have run interference, so to speak, for the idea of progress by humbling the pretensions of the ancients to absolute supremacy in all things; the cycle could, moreover, be optimist as well as pessimist, with an emphasis on renewal rather than decay. But the idea of eternal vicissitudes nonetheless remained the dominant expression of philosophical history in the Renaissance, as it did well into the eighteenth century.

The origins of the idea of secular progress have often been

---

[22] Giordano Bruno, *Des fureurs héroïques* (*De gl' heroici furori*, 1585), edited and translated by Paul-Henri Michel (Paris, 1954), p. 165.
[23] Bruno, *La Cena de le Ceneri*, p. 90.

pushed too far back in time, usually on the basis of a few engaging images pulled out of context. When for more than five hundred years a succession of writers from John of Salisbury through Isaac Newton keep repeating that dwarfs on the shoulders of giants can see further than the giants, they are not committing themselves to the idea of progress in a nineteenth-century sense. It was always recognized that the ancients were the giants and the moderns were the dwarfs. And often as not the image could be turned to the disadvantage of the moderns, as when Sir William Temple caustically wrote: "Let it come about how it will, if we are dwarfs, we are still so, though we stand upon a giant's shoulders; and even so placed, yet we see less than he, if we are naturally shorter sighted, or if we do not look as much about us, or if we are dazzled with the height, which often happens from weakness either of heart or brain."[24]

[24] Sir William Temple, *An Essay upon the Ancient and Modern Learning,* in *Works* (Edinburgh, 1754), II, 159.

4

Man Is a Crooked Stick:
Kant and the Debate on Moral Destiny

IN THE FALL of 1798, when Immanuel Kant was already an old man, a curious work of his, *The Disputation of the Faculties*, was printed in Halle. This was made possible by the felicitous demise of King Frederick William II, whose censor had previously refused an imprimatur to one part of the little book entitled: "Is the human species in continuous progress toward the better?" In a few brilliant pages of the essay, Kant posed the critical problems of historical prediction and, in passing, unwittingly provided us with a convenient framework for an examination of the debate on moral progress in one of its most original forms—the German Enlightenment. He acknowledged three current popular hypotheses with respect to philosophical history and the future moral nature of man: "Either mankind," he writes, "is in continual regression toward the worse, or in constant progression toward the better in its moral destiny; or it remains forever at a standstill on its present level of moral worth among the parts of creation (which is tantamount to an everlasting circular motion around the same point)."[1] And for the three contending parties Kant invented a rather intriguing, though formidable, nomenclature which can be accepted for purposes of this lecture, though I hope his spirit will not condemn too harshly a latitudinarian use of his recondite terminology. The first he called "moral terrorism,"

[1] Immanuel Kant, *Der Streit der Facultäten* (Königsberg, 1798), pp. 134–35.

the second "eudaemonism," and the third "abderitism." Though I shall not adhere to his order, it will be my purpose to illustrate these three divergent positions in eighteenth-century German thought. Ultimately, let me assure you, I shall come back to Immanuel Kant and to his image of man as a crooked stick, or warped timber, which appears in his essay on cosmopolitan history and which I borrowed for my title.

I

Kant used "moral terrorism" to denote an orthodox Protestant theological view of the historical world, which frightened mankind with a prophecy of increasing corruption reaching a climax in the appearance of the anti-Christ. At intervals this conception had gripped large segments of the Protestant world and doubtless was still held by a substantial body of literate pious people in eighteenth-century Germany. While Kant's category of "moral terrorism" was meant to be strictly religious, limited to the apocalyptic preachers, I am extending its scope to include a number of secular versions of the theory which enjoyed great vogue among German intellectuals. To the extent that Stoicism was a frequent moral posture, the belief was widely entertained that the good principle in nature suffered exhaustion, making steady deterioration and ultimate cosmic catastrophe inevitable. The pessimist tenor of the doctrine, often supported by contemporary geological studies of ancient physical upheavals on the planet (a popular form of eighteenth-century science), was at least psychologically akin to theological moral terrorism. In both instances there is constant decay and mankind lives in the shadow of growing moral evil.

An even more generally accepted theory of degeneration was available to Germans in one interpretation of Rousseau's writings. It has often enough been noticed that Rousseau's influence was far more pervasive among German intellectuals of stature than among the French. Jean-Jacques is good litmus paper for testing the underlying temper of a German eighteenth-century thinker, or of any man. Selecting one of the many faces of Jean-Jacques to attack or defend becomes a method of self-identification. In this context the real meaning of Rousseau is beside the point. The two *Discourses* were commonly read in Germany as a history of man's moral fall from the state of nature, a decline that inevitably accompanied the progress of the arts and sciences, the growth of technology, the increase of competitive pride, the accumulation of instruments of domination, and the spread of luxury, softness, and effeminacy.

There was much in the German intellectual climate that rendered "moral terrorism," to preserve Kant's phrase, appealing, for here elements of traditional Protestant theology and nascent Gallophobia coalesced. The relative backwardness of the Germans in the arts and sciences, in the material triumphs of civilization, became more tolerable if the much-vaunted French successes could be associated with sin by the religious and with corruption by the secular moralists. The invasion of German princely courts by French fops and adventurers, of German academies of learning by highly remunerated French scientists, aroused natural envy and hostility, and there was some comfort for the despised German intellectual in bewailing the foreign intrusion with the time-worn platitudes of *O tempora! O mores!* There is hardly a major German writer of this period who does not echo, at least in one of his moods, the Rousseauist theme of universal moral declension as it was set forth in the *Discourses*.

For Kant, indefinite retrogression was an untenable philosophical position, because if the movement toward the worse really persisted, mankind would at some point destroy itself. He rejected the argument that degeneration could be proved by the universal consensus of contemporaries lamenting the decline in moral behavior. The reverse was probably true. Mankind, having risen to a higher plateau of self-reformation, could gaze further ahead, and the very prospect of future improvement heightened public criticism of the present state. There is even a hint of the idea, which Freud would have approved, that a growing self-accusation, far from being a sign of decadence, is an inevitable complement of the moralization of mankind. "Our self-censure," Kant writes, "becomes always stronger, the more steps of morality we have already ascended in the whole course of the world, with which we are become acquainted."[2]

II

If Kant could dismiss out of hand the retrogressionists and the moral terrorists, he had to take more seriously the hypothesis of abderitism, a category to which he reverted again and again in his minor works to describe theories of historical oscillation and circularity. Why he used the conceit abderitism is somewhat perplexing. The Abderites were known in antiquity for their foolish and frenzied behavior. The German novelist Christoph Martin Wieland had written a popular *History of the Abderites* in which he related that after a performance of Euripides' *Andromeda* the whole town of Abdera went about obsessively repeating its verses. This is Kant's probable source, for he uses the phrases "busy stupidity" and "empty business" as summations of the abderite history of man. Then again, I fancy that there may be an echo of the Democritan idea of the "whirl" in the term, for Democritus was the most famous citizen of ancient Abdera.

It was Kant's judgment that the abderite position enjoyed a plurality of voices among his contemporaries, and although

2 Kant, "On the Popular Judgment: That may be Right in Theory, but Does not Hold Good in Praxis," in *Essays and Treatises on Moral, Political, and Various Philosophical Subjects,* I (London, 1798), 218.

this is a statistic well beyond verification, I should like, on purely impressionistic grounds, to hazard the opinion that Kant was probably right. Abderitism counted some of the best minds of the age in its ranks. A division should perhaps be made between those who saw nothing but moral flux and reflux, a sort of historical alternation of good and evil, and those who developed more intricate cyclical patterns; but for our purposes the broader category will hold.

Johann Gottfried Herder, who, as we shall see, was in one of his phases an opponent of abderite circularity, was bitterly eloquent in presenting this view in order to demolish it. In an early work on the philosophy of history, he dramatized the hollowness of those who, having denied the historical vision of a general improvement of the world, could find nothing better than "eternal revolution: weaving and unraveling—the labor of Penelope. ... Doubt in a hundred guises, but all with the flashy title 'based on world history'!"[3] In a few pages of his *Letters for the Advancement of Humanity*, written toward the end of his career, an imaginary abderite debunker of the idea of progress levels so devastating an onslaught against it that one almost begins to doubt where Herder really stood on what he called this "major question." Both Herder and Kant conducted strange and ambivalent discussions about moral progress with themselves as well as with known antagonists. They grappled with the idea like Protestant divines in spiritual anguish. Never do you sense in the writings of either of them the self-assured confidence of a Turgot or a Condorcet. And when they have reached their conclusion on the side of the angels—supporting some conception of progress—one is never quite certain whether the imaginary interlocutor who was nominally defeated is not actually the winner. While Herder never fell into the abderite abyss, he obviously hovered on the brink.

---

[3] Johann Gottfried Herder, *Auch eine Philosophie der Geschichte zur Bildung der Menschheit. Beytrag zu vielen Beyträgen des Jahrhunderts* (Riga, 1774), pp. 60–61.

Contemplate history, says Herder's dark alter ego, and what do you see? Plenty of blind passion. Do you also recognize enlightened reason, wisdom, and goodness increasing with the movement of time? To be sure, the human species pushes along chronologically and genealogically, but rationally, morally? What does perfectibility mean? Does it imply the morally better? Is mankind better in its natural inclinations? In the use of moral principles for the ordering of its inclinations? Better in curbing the passions? Better in the exercise of the more difficult virtues? Biologically, man is fixed. There is no prospect of an increase in his powers because their limits have been set by nature. The idea that man might become a superman is not even worthy of discussion. But what about the multiplication of instruments that supplement human strength? In themselves the engines that increase power do not promise moral perfection, because the crucial issue remains: to what uses will these new tools be put?[4] An augmentation of power is in itself neutral; if harnessed to evil it merely strengthens man's capacity for evil. Well, perhaps we need this ideal of progress in order not to fall back into nothingness. Man must talk himself into the belief in progress merely in order to sustain himself on the same moral level. The result is pitiful. "He goes around in circles like the blind horse in the mill."[5] Since the whole exists only in its parts, what can the transcendent advance of mankind possibly mean? "The growing perfection of the whole," Herder's abderite mocks, "might be an ideal that refers to no one in particular. Well, perhaps it exists only in the mind of God, in the Spirit of the Creator. Now what would He be wanting with that kind of toy?"[6] Thus did Herder play devil's advocate—all too convincingly—against the idea of progress.

The Berlin philosopher Moses Mendelssohn was a man

---

[4] Herder, *Briefe zu Beförderung der Humanität,* II (Riga, 1793), 102.
[5] *Ibid.,* II, 105.
[6] *Ibid.,* II, 104.

whom Kant respected and he praised his works; but Kant had to cast him into the abderite limbo. For Mendelssohn in his *Jerusalem* (1783), a work that had an enormous influence in defining what was purportedly the position of Judaism on a variety of things, had taken issue with Lessing's posthumous aphorisms on *The Education of the Human Race*. Mendelssohn had delivered himself of a succinct refutation of the idea that there was any such thing as education of the entire human race for the better. In morality and in religion—and these were for him essentially the same—mankind as a whole remained more or less unchanged through the ages. Progress and moral development were applicable solely to individuals; religious education was limited to a man's life span and was not cumulative for the race. Reluctantly Mendelssohn conceded that there might occur minor fluctuations in public behavior, that there could be some temporary improvement; but after a brief time virtue and vice would again be redistributed in their customary proportions.[7]

When Justus Möser, the redoubtable *Advocatus Patriae*, upon perusing old records discovered that certain heinous crimes which once had been common were now rare, like Mendelssohn he too refused to believe that men had become fundamentally more virtuous; Möser's reflection was at once abderite and psychological. The passions, he wrote, had merely selected a more genteel way for their breakthrough. German classicists of an even more skeptical turn of mind than Mendelssohn or Möser clothed the same idea in traditional allegories—Ixion's wheel or the myth of Sisyphus. Georg Christoph Lichtenberg, who despite his skepticism and relativism had a genuine commitment to the worth of scientific knowledge that is rare among German intellectuals of the period, composed beautifully chis-

---

[7] Moses Mendelssohn, *Jerusalem, a Treatise on Ecclesiastical Authority and Judaism* (1783), translated by M. Samuels (London, 1838), II, 100–101.

eled aphorisms on the insurmountable limits of intellectual and moral advancement. "We must not believe, when we make a few discoveries in this field or that, that this process will just keep going on forever. The high-jumper jumps higher than the plowboy, and one high-jumper better than another, but the height which no human can jump over is very small."[8]

Intellectually by far the strongest holdout against the idea of progress is found among those German thinkers who likened history to a life cycle or to any circular movement in nature. Here we recognize a prolongation of the Renaissance vicissitudes theme. The basic model for this German cycle theory in modern times was Johann Joachim Winckelmann's history of ancient art, a work that had an interesting fortune. The manuscripts show that Winckelmann's original idea was probably derived from Montesquieu's *Grandeur and Decadence of the Romans*. Thus a modern French paradigm for Roman political history was adapted to art history. Then, in turn, the circular pattern of art history in Greece, from primitivism through decadence, was taken over from Winckelmann by Herder and applied to the life span of the whole of a culture anywhere in the world. The groundwork for this crucial expansive innovation in cyclical theory, which sets it off sharply from the earlier writings that had concentrated on the state rather than the culture as the universe of discourse, was laid by Winckelmann when he associated a culture's moral values with its aesthetic ones and maintained that their two cycles invariably pursued a parallel course. The consequences for German philosophical history were revolutionary: since both morals and art were henceforth conceived as equivalent expressions of the same cultural moment, if you branded as decadent a form such as late Hellenistic art, you had by that declaration alone uttered a

[8] Georg Christoph Lichtenberg, *The Lichtenberg Reader*, translated and edited by F. H. Mautner and Henry Hatfield (Boston, 1959), p. 69.

moral condemnation of the whole epoch in which it was created.

In Herder as in Winckelmann, the phases of the culture cycle, at once moral and aesthetic, can be simply set forth. Each people has an original genius. The early form-giving moment in its history is the creative one, though there are virtues in maturity. Exhaustion inevitably follows as a consequence of overcomplexity, the extravagant piling on of the superfluous. And finally there is death. This idea of the culture cycle ultimately became a fixed element in German conceptualizations of the philosophy of history from Hegel through Spengler, and many contemporary academic disciplines are still in its toils.

III

The third view of world history, which Kant labeled eudaemonism, the belief that there is a growth or progress in happiness, was closest to the eighteenth-century French. But no sooner is the category established than one is plunged into the millennium-old controversy: What is this happiness toward which man is advancing? Is it Platonic, Aristotelian, or Epicurean? In eighteenth-century German thought, progress in happiness became a rich and subtle conception, perhaps the center of the debate on moral destiny. Here the philosophies of Leibniz, Herder, and Lessing form a historical unity with a commitment to eudaemonism that was a major challenge to Immanuel Kant.

Leibniz's *Essays on the Theodicy* (1710)—the only one of his writings to enjoy a European reputation in the eighteenth century—presents problems of interpretation. There are passages indicating that all forms of being are in a state of continual progression toward perfection. But in general he seems to feel that the totality of moral good and necessary evil in the world is at all times relatively constant. Events in the world past and future, present and remote, were so inextricably inter-related that the problem of good and evil could be judged only from the vantage point of the completely fulfilled historical design of Providence. Any partial view to the effect that the world was making progress toward the good chronologically seems to be without meaning, because what was at one moment designated as evil in the eyes of men might be necessary for the universal harmony and the ultimate emergence of particular goods. If one surveyed the whole of history, the world at any given time was the optimum creation in its totality and in its particularity; in the myriad connexities of things there was no need to demonstrate a progression from the less good to the better.

But strangely enough, Leibniz's numerous manuscripts on the advancement of science, not published until the nineteenth century, mark him as one of the earliest believers in the possi-bility of real progress in human happiness. These are the pol-icy statements of an activist engaged in convincing the scien-tists and potentates of Europe to undertake specific projects. Throughout, he emphasizes the practical nature of his plans and contrasts them with the impractical eudaemonist utopias of the sixteenth century—those of Thomas More, Tommaso Campanella, and Francis Bacon. Progress is not yet a scientific law of history as it was to become in Condorcet, but many of the constituent elements of the idea are already cropping up. The same theme is not renewed with equal vigor in European thought until Turgot's *Discourses* and Diderot's optimist writ-ings for the *Encyclopedia*.

In Leibniz the multiplication of scientific works still has a strong religious motivation: to achieve a more penetrating knowledge of the universe is a way of glorifying the Creator. But there is at the same time beginning to emerge an appreci-ation of mundane things, of the utility of scientific investigation both for the ordering of society and for the happiness of mankind. And the two are interrelated. To augment the conveniences of life was a practical demonstration of the goodness of God who had intended man to have *bonheur*, Leibniz said when he wrote in French, to be *glückselig*, when he wrote in German. The Leibnizian concept, though it places greater worth on intellectual perfectibility, does not exclude sensate happiness. The eradication of poverty and the elimination of suffering are not yet conceived as humanitarian ends in themselves; they are subordinate to other goals such as the peace, power, and prosperity of the dynastic state, which provides for the proper disposition of God's world. But no longer is there an exclusive concentration upon the Deity. Leibniz has begun to look two ways: both to God and to His creatures. It is within the power of man through the development of scientific institutions to become happier, and in so doing he will serve God.

Leibniz's concept of progress does not yet have the essential attribute of inevitability that it acquired in late eighteenth-century France. He had great fears about another decline into barbarism. Since the organization of science was tied to the power of the monarch, Leibniz could imagine the accumulated knowledge of Europe falling into the hands of obscurantist military leaders, as it had before in China and in Rome. He was even more troubled by dissension among his contemporaries over the methodology of science, which generated confusion, caused experimental waste, and led to the acceptance of false principles. Though on balance he was of the opinion that the European storehouse of knowledge was not likely to be wholly destroyed, human will had to intervene and positive organized action was imperative to prevent regression. His plans for the establishment of academies of learning in Russia and Germany, his efforts toward a union of the churches, and his preoccupation with the conversion of China were all part of his grand design for the safeguarding of science on a world-wide scale in order to protect mankind from a relapse. Neither for Herder, nor for Lessing, nor even for Kant, did the promotion of science and its application ever play as commanding a role in moral progress as they had with Leibniz. The moral worth of science as an ideal was not generally appreciated in the eighteenth-century Germanic world.

German progressist philosophies of history later in the century may have derived from Leibniz, but they introduced a new intellectual twist into his argument. Lessing and Herder, his two major continuators, in revealing the providential design, invented the idea of a world-historical progressive plan gradually unfolding itself throughout all time as a significant demonstration of the goodness of God, a new version of the theodicy. For Lessing the idea of human striving in time became a proof of divine beneficence, because it allowed man the glory of fashioning himself. His *Education of the Human Race*, already noticed in connection with Joachimism, and his freemasonic addresses became eudaemonist manifestoes of the German Enlightenment, the prototype for stadial theories of progress in three leaps, which in the nineteenth century proliferated in the German world. For Lessing the transformations of man are explicitly those of the inner man; they are primarily soul metamorphoses that color all being in each of the three stages. The stadial process is one of extension as well as transformation. At first Revelation involves only Jews; then Christians; finally, in the third stage, it encompasses all mankind. The first relies on material rewards and punishments in this world—the rod is all too often visible in the hand of Jehovah. In Christianity, judgment is more spiritualized—rewards and punishments are postponed to the next world and morality is not dependent upon the immediate experience of pains. The third stage is the internalized reign of moral reason totally free from restraints either now or in the hereafter.[9] Only in his last aphorisms did Lessing face the critical problem of precisely how individual moral education could ever be translated into the education of mankind—the very point that caused Mendelssohn to doubt the reality of progress for the race. As a solution, if he is read literally, Lessing resorted to a theory of metempsychosis, which it is difficult to take seriously and which has left the commentators at loggerheads.

Of the major thinkers after Leibniz, only Wieland seems to approximate the French notion of *bonheur*, a state of controlled pleasurableness, the condition Thomas Jefferson had in mind when he made a revolution to insure the "pursuit of happiness." Wieland usually says "yea" to the pleasures of civilization, its comforts, its arts, and its sciences; in the French optimist manner he looks toward a full emotional and intellectual existence, and he does not concern himself too deeply about the comparative worth of happiness of the mind and happiness of the senses. Other optimist German-speaking writers like the Basel official Isaak Iselin and Carl Friedrich Flögel also contributed their mite to the propagation of a belief in the advantages of the progress of what they called human understanding and to a condemnation of Rousseau, but I have found the content of their works to be completely exhausted in their titles.

IV

At this point the ambiguities of Herder's philosophy of history can no longer be avoided. His former professor at Königsberg, Immanuel Kant, considered him a eudaemonist, but Herder

---

[9] Gotthold Ephraim Lessing, *Die Erziehung des Menschengeschlechts* (1780), in *Sämmtliche Schriften*, edited by Karl Lachmann, 3d edition, revised by Franz Muncker, XIII (Leipzig, 1897), 413–36; *Ernst und Falk. Gespräche für Freymäurer* (1778), in *Sämmtliche Schriften*, XIII, 339–68.

remains by far the most difficult thinker of the German Enlightenment to pigeonhole. There are instances where he seems to be switching sides in the course of a largish paragraph. If some parts of the late *Letters for the Advancement of Humanity* show a consistency with his early essay, *Another Philosophy of History*, this is merely the consequence of his having reversed himself twice in the interim. Even when he tells us dogmatically that there is growth in humanity, his writing is, shall we say, not exemplary in Cartesian clarity. This is Herder's weakness, but also his strength; in the course of giving utterance to all things he does say many profound ones. His philosophy of history, communicated in a thousand different guises but above all in the *Ideas on the Philosophy of History of Mankind*, published in separate sections from 1784 through 1791, was one of the most potent intellectual forces of modern times east of the Rhine—in the Slav as well as in the German worlds. It became the Bible of nationalism and nationalist history in Eastern Europe.

Humanity must achieve plenitude in time—this is for Herder the fulfillment of God's plan. If there were a possible form of humanity, a cultural embodiment in a *Volk* character, that failed of realization, it would imply a derogation of God's perfection and His goodness. The optimum world in the Leibnizian sense is for Herder a world that in the course of history brings into actuality all possible cultural configurations, like all possible chords on a harp. There is no gradation of excellence among them; they are all different and none are really comparable.

Now if we ask straightforwardly, "Is a later chronological stage of mankind in any way preferable to an earlier one?" it is virtually impossible to get a yes-or-no answer from Herder. Since the emergence of all or virtually all forms of cultural being sometime and somewhere is necessary for the completion of the providential design, ideas of superiority and inferiority have no relevance. Surely nothing has surpassed the youth of mankind that was Greece—or excelled Hebrew poetry. Later nations, which are cognizant of the existence of earlier ones, may derive inspiration from the glorious creations of the past, but inspiration does not mean imitation because each *Volk* genius is so unique that it cannot risk mimesis without self-destruction.

And yet at times Herder did discern signs in European society that mankind was in fact making progress in an absolute sense. Here the concept of humanity has a somewhat different meaning: men were becoming milder, gentler, more loving toward one another, more humane, workmanlike, and industrious, less cruel, bellicose, and glory-seeking. Many passages applaud the development of the middle-class virtues of order, tolerance, activity, and tranquility in a manner that was common among his British and French contemporaries. But while French philosophers of history saw this growth in humanity as bound up with the progress of technical scientific knowledge and the birth of what they named the social and moral sciences, which were havens of certitude, in Herder humanity has no such necessary connection with science. Humanity is a feeling, not a law. Somehow the moral sense of fellow-feeling called humanity is growing and will ultimately possess the world. When Goethe was confronted by this intoxicating prospect of universal love encompassing the race, this knower of men delivered himself of one of those magisterial predictions which catch us up short. After his friend Herder published the third part of his *Ideas*, Goethe wrote from Naples on May 27, 1787: "No doubt he has demonstrated in a superb manner the beautiful dream-wish of mankind that things shall go better with it. I too must admit that I hold it for a truth that humanity will finally be victorious. Only I fear that at the same time the world will become one great hospital in which we behave toward one another like benign male nurses."[10]

If humanity is difficult of definition in the variety of Herder's uses, inhumanity is not. Above all it means war and cruelty. But here one must distinguish between the nature of Kant's and of Herder's antagonism to war, because it colors their divergent concepts of progress. Kant needed eternal peace as a prerequisite for the establishment of a just civil constitution both within a state and in international relations, so that men might perhaps begin to grow morally under law. He saw in war a monstrous violation of the categorical imperative. Since the moral law was absolute and universal, there could not be a double standard: a man could not be moral within his state society if outside it he was called upon to kill in wars between the states. Kant loathed war as destructive of the possibility of man's ever becoming a moral person.

Herder is more grieved by the tragic fate of cultures—not of the individual — under the impact of war and conquest. Among the most moving sections of his masterpiece on the philosophy of history is his portrayal of the stifling of national genius when a more powerful alien horde invades or infiltrates a "natural people." To Herder the occupation of more "backward" and primitive societies was the great historic crime of modern times. No people could ever be assimilated by another. When nations are overwhelmed, the original genius of both conquerors and conquered is suffocated. The victors are corrupted by their new position as overlords; the slaves, who are forced to imitate the customs and manners of their new masters, submit to the destruction of their *Volk* genius. When Herder sees a *Volk* nipped in the bud, he is confronted by religious evil, because a potential divine form of humanity has not been

[10] Johann Wolfgang Goethe, *Die Italienische Reise. Die Annalen* (Zurich, 1950), p. 362.

allowed to flower, to mature, and to live out its natural life cycle. Once again Herder's progress in humanity is sharply at variance with the French *progrès*. De Brosses, Condorcet, and Saint-Simon thought of the forced conversion of savage peoples from fetishistic superstition to scientism as an incontestable, positive good. Herder, on the other hand, bemoaned as absolute evil the extinction of a particular manifestation of humanity in any tribe, however primitive, that was subjected to this "civilizing" process.

Herder's metaphorical attempts to characterize the course of human progress are mixed and contradictory. In his early essay in philosophical history the chain of cultural development from the Tigris-Euphrates valley through contemporary Europe was continuous and each civilization was likened to one of the ages of man. Egypt was the boyhood of mankind as Greece was the handsome youth. In the *Ideas* a major leap of mankind is compared to the metamorphosis of the groveling caterpillar into the liberated butterfly. Then again, the history of each *Volk* is translated into a separate human life cycle from birth to death, and history pullulates with cultures coming into being and passing away. Many of these similes were already hackneyed in Herder's day. Strange as it may seem, it is in the inchoate *Letters for the Advancement of Humanity* that Herder offers what is in my judgment his most original historical model for progress. Emancipated from trite stadial analogies he adventures with a provocative pattern of philosophical history in which a stubborn belief in the progress of humanity is combined with a startling conception of the jagged, irregular, discontinuous, even antithetical, rhythm of human events: "The line of progress should be conceived as neither straight nor uniform, for it proceeds in all directions, contains all possible twists and angles. The course of nature cannot be adequately rendered by asymptotes, nor an ellipse, nor a spiral. Now man's curiosity fixes on a certain object; again halfway through his investigation he drops it, either because he has become tired of it or because he has been attracted by something different and more novel. After a while when the new object loses its novelty he returns to the former. Or perhaps the pursuit of the second object leads him back to the first.... This results in a contest (*Wettkampf*) of human powers, which are forever increased as the sphere of knowledge and of experience expands."[11] This last version of Herder's world philosophy of history may be somewhat syncopated, but it is still progressive.

v

As if I were a true abderite of the circular persuasion, I now finally return to the great philosopher with whom I began— Immanuel Kant. Kant's was the most famous Enlightenment version of the idea of progress, its culmination, but his views have sometimes been vulgarized to the point where they approximate a Victorian faith in the prospect of an ever rosier and plumper hedonist future. My reading of Kant is quite different: he had a far more complicated outlook, touched by a tragic sense. Having identified the three current models of world history, moral terrorism, abderitism, and eudaemonism, he rejected all of them. A theory of retrogression he associated with religious obscurantism. The circular theory of the abderites was dismissed as unworthy of the dignity of man, as making a marionette show of life. But neither could he join ranks with those who saw history as a progression toward happiness resulting from a change for the better in human nature. The portions of good and bad intermingled in every man could not be altered. Moreover, happiness as the end of man, either the French sensate *bonheur* or the more spiritualized *Glückseligkeit* of Lessing and Herder, was a false end.

---

[11] Herder, *Briefe zu Beförderung der Humanität*, II, 113–14.

Kant's sketch for a cosmopolitan world history exploded this
illusion. If the end of man were happiness, he might better
have been left in Arcadia. Kant was equally scornful of Herder's belief that each culture bore within it the seed of its own
particular form of happiness to nurture and bring to fruition.
In a slashing and often unfair review of his former pupil's
work, Kant pointedly asked: "Does the author really mean
that even if the happy inhabitants of Tahiti, never visited by
more civilized people, were destined to live in peaceful in-
dolence for thousands of centuries, a satisfactory answer could
be given to the question of why they exist at all, and whether
it would not have been just as well if this island had been popu-
lated with happy sheep and cattle, as by human beings happy
in mere sensual pleasure?"[12] Kant understood nature's purpose
for man: the development of all human capabilities beyond the
instinctual. This was called Reason and by definition excluded
what was generally considered sensate happiness. The gratification of the passions, which most men sought, was mere ani-
malian activity.

How then could Kant conceive of or demonstrate any movement toward the better? He tried various ways of convincing
himself as well as his public, and one sometimes has the feeling
that the elements of doubt are getting stronger as he grows
older—though he clung to his belief until his dying day.

In the essay on cosmopolitan history Kant describes a mecha-
nism that is akin to the cunning of reason: the faculties beyond
the instinctual develop as a consequence of the antagonism
(Kant uses the English word) between elements of sociability
and asociability. And he foresees that the next step will be the
institution of a just civil constitution and the establishment of

---

[12] Kant, "Rezensionen von J. G. Herders Ideen zur Philosophie der Geschichte der
Menschheit" (1785), edited by Artur Buchenau and Ernst Cassirer, in *Werke*, IV
(Berlin, 1913), 199.

universal peace. This idea he later expanded in his book on *Perpetual Peace*, a work responsible more than any other for his enrollment among the simplistic philanthropic progressists. But even in his work of the 1780's there are already misgivings. Who will guard the guardians in the future, more ethical, social state? What will happen to man when the stimulus of antagonism is weakened? What evidence is there that the change in political forms must actually lead to more moral conduct, a repression of man's instinctual aggressive behavior? The answers are not readily forthcoming.

In other works the arguments supporting Kant's prediction that men will conduct themselves more ethically in the future are set forth mostly with negative rhetoric. And as for the last essay, *The Disputation of the Faculties*, it takes a confirmed nineteenth-century progressist to read into it the sanguine assurance that Kant never had. For Kant there is no real empirical proof that moral progress will be continuous in the future. He is not one to extrapolate a curve; quite on the contrary, on empirical grounds he can always envisage the possibility of a *punctum flexus contrarii* in either direction, progression or retrogression.

At most, Kant offers a glimmer of hope that there is in man an inclination toward the good. And what is his evidence? Men everywhere, he says in 1798, have voiced enthusiasm for the republican form of government established by the French Revolution. They have thus indicated an awareness that they have a right to rule themselves. And if republican forms prevail, then wars will, *ex hypothesi*, end, because only monarchs, not peoples, have an interest in waging them. This answer is less a philosophical demonstration than an outburst of defiance against Prussian monarchical authority, which had restricted Kant's freedom of publication. In Kant the enthusiasm for the French Revolution is not founded upon any certainty that this revolution will necessarily succeed; he is fully aware that it may well degenerate into chaos. Sympathy for the Revolution is merely a symptom of a human tendency. There is no sturdy conviction of continuous moral progression. The good and moral societal arrangement that will make men act ethically may turn up some time since the tendency potentially exists. "When" is a problem subject to the laws of probability, he says. Perhaps after many terrible trials.

For Kant the idea of progress sometimes has the quality of an undemonstrable article of faith; man must believe in it because the hapless creature, a "crooked stick" he calls him, needs this crutch in order to have the courage to exist. If men could not find solace in the prospect for betterment, the horrible spectacle of the world would drive them to give up the fight. Even if the activists among them carried on, for they were players on the world stage and hence by definition fools, the rational observers at least would have to surrender in despair. Kant the moralist delivered a sermon to buck up faltering humanity: You have no right to abdicate, since you can never be sure that progress is not a reality; it is your duty, your inborn duty, to act *als ob*—as if progress were indeed determined. This is a far cry from the assured, self-satisfied, complacent nineteenth-century feeling with which the term progress came to be associated. Kant's belief in progress recalls the scene of a skeptic on his death-bed, argued into the sacrament of extreme unction. Take it, how do you know? Maybe progress does exist after all. What is there to lose morally? It is a secular version of Pascal's wager.

What is the hope of the world? asks Kant toward the end of his life. The sheer increasing destructiveness of war may force mankind toward the better. Only this heroic remedy prevents Kant from despairing of the future of humanity. This is the kind of last-ditch belief in progress we in our times can understand from bitter experience. The Victorians could not.

Perhaps the best way finally to dispel the image of Kant as a starry-eyed progressist free from doubt is to turn to the conclusion of the second part of his *Disputation of the Faculties,* a piece whose corrosive humor has not always been appreciated, least of all by the Germans themselves. He tells there of a patient whose doctor comforted him day after day with remarks of growing signs of betterment. When visited by a friend who asked him how he was getting on, the sick man replied: *"Ich sterbe für lauter Besserung*—I am dying from sheer improvement."[13]

[13] Kant, *Der Streit der Facultäten*, p. 161.

5

Taming the Future:
The French Idea of Perfectibility

I n 1765 there appeared under an Amsterdam imprint a work by a certain Abbé Bazin with the novel title *La Philosophie de l'histoire*. It was probably the first use of this particular combination of words as the formal subject of a book, though as far back as 1566 the political theorist Jean Bodin had employed the term *philosophistoricus* in characterizing Philo the Jew.[1]

The Abbé Bazin's work was a most inauspicious beginning for the presentation of a form of knowledge that for two centuries has consistently irritated and sometimes outraged empiricist historians. It was really no more than a pamphlet of about 200 pages and dealt mostly with the history of antiquity, raising such disturbing questions as whether Moses was not really Bacchus in disguise. Its pretentious title was no more warranted than was its grandiloquent dedication to the Empress of Russia. Moreover, to compound its many blasphemies and historical inaccuracies, it was not written by the Abbé Bazin at all, but by none other than Monsieur Arouet de Voltaire, up to his old tricks of ascribing militantly critical and anti-theological propositions to a deceased cleric who had been known for his piety. The title of Voltaire's book took hold, and for better or for worse philosophies of history henceforth ceased to be mere-

---

[1] Bodin, *Methodus*, p. 447. In the *Avis des Editeurs* of the Geneva 1756 edition of Voltaire's *Essay sur l'histoire générale, et sur les moeurs et l'esprit des nations, depuis Charlemagne jusqu'à nos jours*, the Cramer brothers called his work an *Histoire Philosophique du Monde*.

ly implicit ideas, buried in writings on theology, morals, and statecraft as they had been in the Western world for more than 2,000 years, and assumed a new status, explicit and self-conscious. Philosophy of history moved from the wings onto the center of the stage and became a discipline in its own right. This is a momentous transformation in the history of any intellectual problem—the act of baptism or naming.

At about the same period, as we saw in the previous lecture, a slew of works began to appear in German calling themselves *Philosophie der Geschichte*. World chronology, which had been the central problem of universal history in the seventeenth century, thus gave way to philosophical history in the eighteenth. For about a century thereafter, roughly from the latter part of the eighteenth through well past the middle of the nineteenth, there was a vast outpouring of grand systems. But while philosophical history enjoyed a general vogue everywhere in Europe, by far the most original writing was heavily concentrated in France and in Germany. The Italian Vico had no important successor in his native land. And in England, except for the rather imitative works of Richard Price and Joseph Priestley in the eighteenth century and Herbert Spencer and Henry Thomas Buckle in the nineteenth, the subject was not seriously cultivated. Since French and German philosophies of history during this period formed cultural personality as well as expressed it, their mood outlasted the age of their composition, and their images, imprinted upon national character, have persisted well into our own day.

I

In France and Germany two separate intellectual chains were established, and there are long parallel developments where influences from one thinker to another can be clearly delineated within each national culture. In the French school the main current ran from Turgot through Condorcet, Saint-Simon, and the Saint-Simonians, culminating in the mammoth structure of Auguste Comte. As individuals these men, spanning three generations, were tied to one another with the iron bonds of discipleship, friendship, or bitter enmity. In Germany a similar line is traceable from Herder, Lessing, and Kant through Fichte and Schelling until it achieved its *summa* in Hegel's lectures at Berlin in the 1820's. Though he was not the first to teach it publicly, Hegel made the philosophy of history academic and himself its paramount interpreter. Through him the subject attained the height of respectability by penetrating the austere chambers of the German state university system. The writings of Karl Marx in the 1840's and '50's are probably more in the German than in the French tradition, though he synthesized elements from both sides of the Rhine, and we shall be treating him as a hybrid.

A word about the autonomous rise of the French and German schools. The very idea of drawing a significant contrast between shapes of philosophical history in two modern European nations divided by nothing more than a river might well be questioned, but the fact is that the schools did evolve in relative intellectual independence. While many theoretical idioms are common to both of them and one could profitably explore the resemblances, the distinctions are striking. In eighteenth-century Europe, when intellectual currents moved from West to East, a group of creative Germans in far-off East Prussia (Kant, Hamann, and Herder) read all the important French books at a time when French thinkers hardly deigned to peruse what any German was publishing. But though Herder and Hegel actually journeyed to Paris, their contact with French thought aroused in them only hostility, negation, and ultimate rejection. If there was any influence, it was *à rebours*. In one of his last lectures on the *Philosophy of History*, Hegel pontifically excommunicated all the Latin nations: "With them the inner life is a region whose depth they do not appreciate, for it is given over 'bodily' to particular absorbing interests, and the infinity that belongs to Spirit is not to be looked for there."[2]

The impact of the German philosophers of history on the French was negligible even in the nineteenth century. By the time Herder, Lessing, and Kant were translated, the foundation and framework of the French structure had already been erected. Though Victor Cousin's lectures on German thought during the last years of the Restoration were fashionable, it is highly dubious whether his much-touted transmission ever really took place. Saint-Simon had made a brief trip to Germany early in the century, but he always spoke ill of the German romantic spirit. When his disciples the Saint-Simonians were forging their doctrine in dramatic closeted debates in 1829 and 1830, the term "Hegelian" was a scornful epithet hurled at metaphysical quibblers. If the Saint-Simonians borrowed the concept of antagonism from Kant's essay on cosmopolitan history, they grafted a completely different meaning onto it. It is reported that Hegel said a few kind words about Auguste Comte to his friend Gustave d'Eichthal and that Comte reciprocated by including a Hegel Day in the Positivist Calendar of Humanity, but that was the extent of their communion.

In this lecture and in the one that follows I shall attempt to illuminate the distinctive characters of the French and German schools. This age of the great systems in philosophical history displayed a brilliant awareness of the problems, an inventiveness, a thematic richness, and a creative originality that render it classical. The influence of these systems quickly overflowed the narrow boundaries of the historical in any professional

---

[2] Georg Wilhelm Friedrich Hegel, *The Philosophy of History*, translated by J. Sibree, revised edition (New York, 1900), p. 421.

sense, and ideas first propounded by Condorcet, Saint-Simon, Comte, Hegel, and Marx have turned up as basic assumptions, not always well labeled, in anthropology, psychology, political thought, sociology, and such other sciences of man as are renamed from time to time in our academic curricula. By contrast with the hoary giants, late nineteeth- and twentieth-century philosophies of history often seem to be the work of industrious epigoni whose writings have crammed the old bins with the harvest of recent historial scholarship, both the chaff and the wheat.

II

And now let us turn to the French.

The French writers who created the major themes of philosophical history were incorrigible activists—a King's minister, Baron Turgot; a leader of the Revolution, Condorcet; founders of movements and new religions, Saint-Simon, Fourier, the Saint-Simonians, Auguste Comte. For them the prospect of implementing their ideas seemed immediate. Saint-Simon on his death-bed exhorted his disciples: "The pear is ripe—pluck it!"[3] They were bringing a new world into being, accelerating the projected rectilinear historical series. It will be readily understood why many of their theories of perfectibility have become virtually official ideology in the dynamic societies on both sides of the Atlantic.

By the time Voltaire popularized the term *philosophy of history*, Turgot had already delivered his famous valedictory addresses before the Sorbonne on the successive "progressions of the human mind," a title that was preserved by his protégé Condorcet in his famous work of 1794, *Sketch of a Historical Survey of the Progressions of the Human Mind*, the canonical eighteenth-century French text on the idea of progress, writ-

[3] *Notice historique*, in *Oeuvres de Saint-Simon et d'Enfantin*, 2d edition, I (Paris, 1865), 121.

ten in the shadow of the guillotine. As if in rebuttal of Montesquieu's anatomy of the fall of Rome, these two optimist philosophers demonstrated that the values of contemporary French scientific and rationalist society would endure forever, growing in strength throughout all time: the modern Antonines would never decline. The thesis was simple. Because of the cumulative effect of scientific knowledge, regression was impossible. The French had already reached a high level of intelligence, and they would scale the still loftier summits ahead with the same facility.

The problem of man had been completely solved for these French eighteenth-century thinkers. Scientific method, now universally appreciated, had projected a roadway into infinity. Progress was irreversible and indefinite, by which Condorcet meant that the future prospects of pleasure and power over nature were so vast that man could not even conceive of them in his imagination until he had climbed to greater heights. By wresting from nature its own secrets, its laws, he wrote in a manuscript, man could eventually tame nature. In the future man would enter the lists an equal in power with nature itself —one of the grandest expressions of hubris in an age not characterized by excessive humility.

What was history for the eighteenth-century French theoretician of progress? It was the record of man's steady conquest of the external world, beginning in a period when he was still the member of a feeble and isolated band, and culminating in his present high estate. In the struggles of the past, victims had fallen by the wayside, but mankind as a whole, always guided by the pain-pleasure principle, had kept fairly well to the main road of progress. Pleasure and desire had led man onward, and so had the mild but necessary irritability responsive to pain. The historical process could be represented as a series of needs, their appeasement, and the creation of new needs in the course

of satisfying the old ones, ad infinitum. In his second Sorbon-
ique Turgot extolled the superiority of the progressive human
and historical over the repetitive natural order of the world.
"The phenomena of nature, subject to constant laws, are enclosed in a circle of revolutions that are always the same. Everything is reborn, everything perishes, and through successive
generations in which vegetation and animal life reproduce
themselves, time merely restores at each instant the image it
has caused to disappear.

"The succession of men, however, presents a changing spectacle from century to century. Reason, the passions, liberty,
produce new events without end. All ages are linked to each
other by a series of causes and effects, which bind the present
state of the world to all those that have preceded it. The conventional signs of language and writing, affording men the
means of maintaining a sure hold on their ideas and of commu-
nicating them to others, have formed of all the special kinds of
knowledge a common treasury, which one generation transmits
to another like a legacy that is ever being augmented with the
discoveries of each century; and thus the human race, considered from its beginnings, appears to the eyes of a philosopher
to be one immense whole that, like every individual, has its
infancy and its progress."[4]

To be sure, an element of conflict had been introduced into
history whenever wicked corps (tyrants, priests, cliques of philosophers) for a time monopolized the instruments of power,
of knowledge, and of pleasure. The corps spirit had suppressed
novelty, Turgot charged in the *Discourses*. But the periods of
stagnation had never endured. Wise and good men successfully
broke the bonds of sameness, gathered fresh impressions, pro-
mulgated new ideas, and found adherents among the rulers

[4] Anne Robert Jacques Turgot, Baron de l'Aulne, *Oeuvres*, edited by Gustave Schelle,
I (Paris, 1913), 214–15.

themselves. For who could long resist the seduction of instrumentalities that promised power and pleasure? Occasionally there were barbarian irruptions from the heart of darkness in the East, but the invaders were quickly assimilated as soon as they acquired the elementary tools of knowledge.

The Marquis de Condorcet, Turgot's successor, writing at a pivotal moment in the history of the idea of progress, posed a momentous question. Would not liberty and free inquiry, which in the past had been the absolute guarantees of progressive development, have to bend a little in the future before the new demands of scientific organization? The past rate of rather haphazard development could in the future be increased to an undreamed-of degree if the practice of science were vested in organized bodies rather than in free-wheeling individual scientists. Hence the impressive catalogue of worldwide controlled researches projected in Condorcet's *Fragment on the New Atlantis*, most of them in our day become laboratory realities. Since each scientific acquisition in the past had ultimately been transmuted into a quantum of pleasure distributed among mankind, what a harvest of well-being and happiness was in store if the accumulative process of science and technology could only be quickened through coordination. Speed of achievement, a sense of urgency, henceforth became a vital ingredient of the idea of progress, for delay was associated with a prolongation of needless suffering for mankind. Condorcet, the doctrinaire liberal in politics, was all too willing to accept the imposition of external discipline on the republic of science for the sake of human betterment. An ominous concession.

The movement of future progress described by Condorcet can be likened to the advance of the whole of mankind on an open plain. In the front rank, ahead of their fellow men, the scientific elite are dashing forward at a pace that is continually accelerated. Behind the main body, portions of humanity lag because they have been duped by Machiavellian despots and their priestly minions. But the forward thrust of the great cohort of scientists is of such Herculean power that it pulls the whole of mankind along with it. And as they advance in time, men are ever healthier, happier, more acute in their sense perceptions, telescopically and microscopically, more precise in their reasoning power, more equal in wealth and opportunity, more humane in their conduct, more moral. "Let us dare to envisage, in the vast prospect of the centuries that will follow us, a happiness and an enlightenment about which we cannot today even form a vague and indefinite idea. Let us count on that perfectibility with which nature has endowed us, on the power of genius from which long experience has taught us to expect prodigies, and let us console ourselves for the fact that we shall not witness those happier times with the pleasure of foretelling them, of enjoying them in advance, and perhaps with the even sweeter satisfaction of having accelerated that all-too-distant epoch by a few moments."[5]

Saint-Simon and Auguste Comte later introduced new dynamic motifs into this easy-flowing history of science and technology, especially the idea of the conflict of classes and the concept of crises. But even in their view of the historical process, the crises were still finite and readily resolved. The standard formula was the defeat or abdication of an old ruling class and its replacement by a new one. Historical crises were primarily extrinsic, the consequence of a mechanical disequilibrium in the manifest organization of civil society, which had failed to take into account the vast accretion of knowledge and power in what were formerly subordinate groups. The ideal historical solu-

[5] Marie Jean Antoine Nicolas Caritat, Marquis de Condorcet, *Vie de Turgot*, in *Oeuvres*, edited by A. Condorcet O'Connor and M. F. Arago, V (Paris, 1847), 224–25. Condorcet identified himself with Turgot's views.

tions were largely institutional: the creation of a new hierarchy, a more reasonable division of labor and power reflecting the new conditions, the elimination of contradictions between civil and political authority.

According to the French school the process of historical change since the beginning of time has been remarkably continuous—perhaps its most significant attribute. A stage or a period in Condorcet's *Sketch* is a step on the ladder of progress that merely punctuates the continuum. The discoveries of genius are great moments in the historical ascent, but they have been prepared by a long series of little steps called gradual development. Historical movement is so inherently continuous that all periodization is in the final analysis arbitrary. One may recall that there are ten epochs in Condorcet's world history, a rational number. How convenient of history to express itself in terms of the metric system! Condorcet's favorite analogy to the historical process is a mathematical progression. Auguste Comte, who periodized history in the famous law of three states, was nevertheless analyzing one long linear "social series"—his term. The same sense of continuous process (without leaps or real disruptions) persisted even after dialectical elements had been added by Saint-Simon, the Saint-Simonians, and Comte. The Saint-Simonian alternation of "organic" and "critical" periods in past history involves merely a normal heartbeat, a systole and a diastole in a constant progressive movement.

As an analogy the mathematical series never lost its fascination. The organic metaphors that Saint-Simon and Comte borrowed from biology could not render the idea of infinity as convincingly as an arithmetic progression without end. In the organic image the fear of death or the notion of mere cyclical recurrence always lurked in the background. Infinite organic growth was hard to imagine, while a long mathematical series moving in one direction and begging for extrapolation was irresistible. Why should the course be reversed? If in the past there had been temporary stoppages and even brief setbacks, the Saint-Simonian theory of continuous progress improvised specific *ad hoc* explanations for what were cavalierly dismissed as insignificant deviations from the main current of history. For the future even these minor aberrations from linear progress were excluded by dogmatic assertion. "The law of perfectibility is . . . absolute," the Saint-Simonians proclaimed in a public lecture in 1829. "Today everything leads to the conclusion that with the cessation of wars, with the establishment of a regime that will put an end to violent crises, no retrogression, not even a partial one, will ever again take place. There will be continuity and acceleration of the progressions among the whole of mankind, for peoples will teach one another and will sustain one another."[6]

In summary the French philosophers of perfectibility were writing histories of progressive happiness and humanity. What there was of a historical drama could be succinctly described as the overcoming of temporary impediments in physical nature and in the residual wicked instincts of man, which would be channeled or atrophied so that increasing happiness might reign unchallenged forever. "The imagination of the poets placed the Golden Age in the cradle of mankind, in the ignorance and brutality of early times. It is rather the Iron Age that should be relegated there. The Golden Age of the human species is not behind us, it is before us," wrote Saint-Simon in one of his early brochures.[7]

---

[6] *Doctrine de Saint-Simon. Exposition. Première année, 1829,* new edition by C. Bouglé and Elie Halévy (Paris, 1924), pp. 166–67.

[7] Henri de Saint-Simon, *De la réorganisation de la société européenne* (1814), in *Oeuvres choisies* (Brussels, 1859), II, 328.

In describing the French proponents of progress, I have perhaps bridged too casually the divide between the eighteenth
and the nineteeth centuries. I should therefore like to accentu-
ate a number of differences between them, especially in their
definitions of the final goal of history. Condorcet, Saint-Simon,
and Comte were all committed to the idea that the long-term
movements of the course of history would show a new man
and a new society inevitably burgeoning out of the past. But
if we refuse to take them at their prophetic word, their formula can be turned around. It is their man of the past who
grows out of the man of the future fixed in their mind's eye.
This citizen of utopia can be established as the starting-point
of their version of the historical process, which then is played
backward, like a film in reverse. After having determined the
character of the harbor where man was destined to find a safe
haven, these reformer-philosophers constructed the route along
which he had come.

True to the romantic spirit of the early nineteenth century,
the philosophers of history who succeeded Turgot and Condorcet abandoned a theory of ideal human nature in which mind
was the supreme universally recognized capacity to which all
other talents were subordinate. Once Saint-Simon, Fourier, the
Saint-Simonians, and Comte defined man as a feeling and willing being whose capacities for love and action were of equivalent, if not superior, worth to his reason, philosophical history
had to be totally reformulated as the progress of love or the
progressive actualization of all three major capacities, instead
of the development of mind alone. The basic model of perfectibility as a measurable extension of human well-being over
ever-broadening areas at an ever-faster tempo was preserved
by this new generation of the French school, but the philo-

sophical historian was now summoned to focus upon an entirely different aspect of human existence—the growth in time of man's affective or emotional nature rather than his reason alone.

Though belief in the inevitability and infinitude of progress was identical with that of the eighteenth-century rationalists, the content of the idea of progress changed. The definition of what was progressing was expanded substantially from the eighteenth to the nineteenth century. In Turgot and Condorcet and the early Saint-Simon the conclusion is inescapable that the history of mankind since primitive times had in fact demonstrated the gradual flowering of rational, abstract capacities at the expense of imaginative and passionate nature, and they deemed this one-sided transformation good because the passions were suspect. The unfortunate primitive, once capable of nothing but concrete perception, had become with time a generalizer, a member of the French Academy of Sciences, and there was every expectation that man's preferred method of communication would become ever more abstract in the future until he talked nothing but pure mathematics.

For the later Saint-Simon and the Saint-Simonians, progress was never encased within the relatively narrow compartment that such a rationalist view pre-established. Theirs was not a world in which you withdrew from the passions what you bestowed upon reason, or a closed economy with a fixed quantum of energy. Saint-Simonian man had infinite potentialities in all directions; he could at one and the same time progress in power over nature, in expansive feeling, and in the endless accumulation of knowledge. Thus the Saint-Simonians rejected the exclusivity and limitations of all previous definitions of man and of perfectibility. The Christian duality of the spiritual and the corporeal, and the contempt of the body and its desires, the eighteenth-century hypertrophy of reason and its implied denigration of the creative imagination, and the Stoic repression of feeling were all banished. Man was both body and soul, loving, insatiably athirst for learning, boundlessly dynamic in his conquests of nature.

Instead of the man of reason as the most perfect expression of humanity, Saint-Simon thinks of man now and in the future as at once rational, activist, and religious. His ends are moral, intellectual, and physical, three major areas of human effort corresponding to the natural aptitudes of the moralist, the scientist, and the administrator. This is the whole man, whose being must find a correspondence in the organization of the healthy society of the future. If man is primarily a rational animal and the highest form of reason is mathematics, the Turgot-Condorcet egalitarian ideal of rational units behaving in accordance with mathematicized social rules is comprehensible. But if humanity is a composite, whose various ideal manifestations include activist and religious as well as rationalist elements, the good social structure should be organismic, a harmony of complex, and different, parts. The organic society, in contrast to the atomist egalitarian society which functions like inanimate clockwork, then cries out for a "vitalist" force—some pervasive emotion, feeling, or belief to give life to the body. Though the eighteenth century had developed the concepts of benevolence and humanity as characteristics of men of natural virtue, Saint-Simon in the romantic temper invested the idea of the love of humanity coursing through the body social with an emotional fervor which is absent in the sober writing of the *philosophes*.

Under the influence of Saint-Simon and that of his followers, a quest for the cohesive organismic forces in all past history was deliberately undertaken. World history became the study of the gradual contraction of the area of antagonism and the diffusion of love in an ever-widening circle from the family to the tribe to the nation to the whole of humanity. This was an adaptation of the spatial imagery that Turgot and Condorcet had once used to describe the slow extension of scientific enlightenment and the gradual blotting out of obscurantism. A history of the expansion of love replaced that of the successive advances of mind. In the hundred years of French philosophical history, Turgot's progress of the human mind was translated into the Saint-Simonian progress of the general actualization of all human capacities.

In its detail Saint-Simonian history is not quite so simple as this image at first implies. While antagonism assumed new shapes—city wars, national wars, religious wars—the old conflicts were not completely eradicated within the inflated structures of association, so that even after international religious societies were organized the spirit of hostility within the family based upon age and sex differences, within the city based upon families, and within the nation based upon cities tenaciously persisted. Love had never taken complete possession of even the most intimate associations of the older "in-groups" —to employ a contemporary barbarism. A Saint-Simonian view of the world as it stood on the threshold of association and love gave rise to the paradoxical reflection that there was still pervasive antagonism throughout human society both on an international and on an intimate personal level; on the verge of universal love, the world was riddled with hates. The conflicts might be said to have diminished within the limits of the smaller associations only in the sense that they had become attenuated and milder in their overt expressions. Men were no longer commonly anthropophagous.

Another facet of antagonism that had undergone a series of quantitative, measurable changes was manifested in the economic exploitation of one man by another, in the treatment of men as objects rather than persons (here the Saint-Simonians clearly drew on Cesare Beccaria and Kant). In the earliest times men devoured their captives, then with progress they merely killed them, and finally they enslaved them. The first modes of the series were lost in pre-history, but the later forms of exploitation were known and recorded in the successive institutions of slavery, serfdom, and free labor. Legally, at every one of the stages, there had been some further limitation upon the absolute power of the exploitation of man by man. The progress of love was thus demonstrable, though complete freedom had not yet been achieved and in the condition of the modern proletariat—the indignity of the term, connoting the status of workers as a mere childbearing mass, made it repugnant to Saint-Simonians—remnants of the ancient forms of exploitation had survived. There were vital respects in which modern workers were still slaves and serfs—a common theme in the contemporary literature depicting the wretchedness of the laboring classes in Western society. But though exploitation was an abominable reality of the organization of work, a review of its history proved that in long terms it was a waning form and that association and sociability were steadily gaining the upper hand.

IV

Like all triadic systems, ancient and modern, the Saint-Simonian doctrine confronted grave problems in positing a final goal for history. The role, relative potency, and position of excellence of the three elements composing the unity of human nature led to acrimonious dispute. What was man after all? Was he primarily a rational, a sentient, or an activist being? Which psychological type should rule in the ideal world of the future? Which should lead in the march of progress and which should docilely accept subordination? The eighteenth-century rationalists had faced none of these troublesome questions because for them the reign of reason, at least as an ideal, was virtually unchallenged. In the end the Saint-Simonians stressed the final phase of their master's thought and elevated to pre-eminence the artists—their generic name for what Saint-Simon in his private lexicon had once called the Platonic capacity—a category that extended far beyond painters, poets, and musicians to embrace all moral teachers and guides, whatever their instruments of instruction. The Saint-Simonians saw the crisis of modern times as an emotional one and the malady of the age as a morbidity of the sentient capacity. Mankind's talent for love had shriveled. It was the hope of the Saint-Simonian movement to restore this capacity to a central position in the progressive education of the future.

Since the sentient capacity was the key to man's religious future, clearly the man of feeling was the ideal personality type before whom his brothers in humanity had to genuflect. Going back into history, the Saint-Simonians discovered that the man of moral capacity, the religious leader, had always set the goals and had inspired others with the desire to achieve them. By his side the rationalist scientist who merely accumulated observations was a glacial, analytic agent, indispensable for progress, but surely not to be ensconced on the throne.

The gospel of Charles Fourier, the *anti-philosophe*, though he does not fit neatly into this intellectual catena, went even further than did the Saint-Simonians in rejecting reason as the end of history. This petty, frustrated clerk, who spent his years in dingy *pensions*, foretold the ultimate triumph of an expansive sensuality, when his system of phalansteries, or communities based on natural and diverse inclinations for work and pleasure, would cover the earth. Man desired not illusory juridical rights or scientific gadgets, but the direct and immediate gratification of the passions. Though civilization had originally been an advance over states of savagery, patriarchy, and barbarism, in its present decadent condition its superiority was not marked enough to attract either savages or barbarians. In the civilized world anarchic competition was despoiling the earth. Men with different passionate natures were constricted within the bonds of monogamous marriage, forcing them to seek their sexual pleasures clandestinely. Men had desires for gastronomic satisfaction, for ever more multifarious luxuries of the table; yet such pleasures were denied to the vast bulk of the population, and the lot of a substantial portion was hunger. And all this in the name of reason and civilization! Since the direct fulfillment of the passions in all their forms, gross as well as sublimated, was the destiny of man according to Fourier, the ascetics, the moralists, and the rationalists of all ages became the evil ones and the libertines the new saints.

Fourier's formulations were so offensive to the society in which he lived that his complex theory of sensate progression has never to my knowledge found a favorable reception among historians. Most liberal progressist history-writing of modern times has of course been inspired by Condorcet; even the Saint-Simonian conception of the progressive enlargement of the orbit of love and association as a shape of philosophical history has won adherents; but alas, a Fourierist history yet remains to be written. I offer this, *en passant*, as a worthwhile challenge to a new generation nurtured on Freud and prepared to recount a history of the id as well as of the superego.

v

The French idea of perfectibility received its final nineteenth-century shape from Auguste Comte, one of the most tragic figures in the history of thought—a psychotic genius who built a grand architectonic structure around the idea of progress during his lucid intervals between bouts with the demons of insanity. His is by far the most magnificent creation of the French school, its climax; but paradoxically it is the closest to the German in form, in content, and in ponderousness.

While there has recently been a renascence of Hegelian philosophy in France, the works of her native son Auguste Comte lie virtually neglected. And yet the parallels between the two systematizations evolved independently on either side of the Rhine are becoming more strikingly evident as time sets them both in perspective. Stripped of the thick hide of their private terminology, these philosophical dinosaurs stand revealed as belonging to the same species.

Comte's Great Being—the opposite number of Hegel's World Spirit—possessed in turn all of the sciences in the encyclopedic hierarchy from astronomy to physics, chemistry, biology, sociology, and finally morality. Each one of these sciences had gone through theological and metaphysical stages before it became positive, and the total experience in one science had been completed before the process could be initiated in its successor, a development that ended with the writing of Comte's treatise on morality. Both systems, the Hegelian and the Comtean, are at once logics and philosophies of history. Both deal with the epistemological relationship between subject and object, and both resolve it by temporalizing the problem.

The distinctive element in the Comtean doctrine that is often neglected is the richness of his psychological characterization of the three progressive historical stages of consciousness. Though he is known as the founder of sociology, Comte's law of the changing nature of psychological perception in time may turn out to be his most original insight. In a revealing and little-noticed excursus in the third volume of his massive *System of Positive Polity,* he reported that during the course of his madness in 1826 he had acquired an intimate personal conviction of the truth of the law of three states. As his illness became aggravated, he had felt himself regress through various stages of metaphysics, monotheism, and polytheism, to fetishism, and then, in the process of recuperation, had watched himself mount again through the progressive changes of human consciousness, at once historical and individual, to positivism and health.[8] This was a far more profound conception than the rather commonplace analogy between phylogeny and ontogeny to which Saint-Simon had regularly alluded. When a man went mad and there was a derangement of psychic processes he naturally fell back along the same historic path of development that the race had once ascended. This embryonic Comtean version of an idea of a collective consciousness, its origins, and growth, and the view of regression as at once a return to the infantile and to the primitive, had many eighteenth-century roots; but never before in the literature of psychology or historical sociology had these ideas been developed with comparable vigor. Comte's own malady had bestowed psychic depth upon an intellectualist conception. The very content and moral tone of his law of the three states was qualitatively different from previous theories of this character.

Comte's immediate French predecessors—Turgot, Condorcet, and Saint-Simon—still believed that in the future a baby emerging from the womb would be fundamentally the same kind of psychological being as it had been in the past and that it would remain so throughout its life. Comte raised the idea of progress to a new level when, in addition to technological, scientific, intellectual, and moral achievement which his predecessors had recognized, he envisaged a progressive growth of consciousness. At the same time he had the extraordinary insight that as mankind advanced, the earlier stages of consciousness would not be completely sloughed off and buried forever, but that, on the contrary, every child born in the new humanity would re-experience the history of the race and pass through its successive states of intelligence in the course of attaining maturity. In previous French stadial theories once a higher

---

[8] Auguste Comte, *Système de politique positive, ou Traité de sociologie, instituant la religion de l'humanité*, III (Paris, 1853), 75–6.

level has been reached the old forms are totally abandoned. The curtain is rung down and a new act begins. For Comte the fetishist world was an ever-present reality, and in his religious philosophy he sought a means of preserving in the positive polity of the future the direct and immediate emotional responses that characterized primitive life.

While Comte was committed to progress as his historical framework, in the second period of his life he became obsessed with the contradictions of order and progress. This was another departure from the eighteenth-century outlook. Turgot had been almost pathologically afraid of sameness and its deadening effect on man and history, but Comte came to see in those who pursued novelty and innovation for their own sake an even greater danger. He raised the specter of formlessness, absence of order, as the new, dread anti-progressist force and established a French sociological tradition that is still reflected in Emile Durkheim's idea of *anomie*. An innovation in science or in political administration, however remarkable, that was not organically integrated with man's affective nature was for Comte destructive of the good order; it was like an act of historical regression either in an individual or in humanity. Throughout his presentation of world history Comte was ever vigilant to single out the violators of the orderly, historical timetable and to censure them retrospectively. Condorcet's goading of science and technology into ever-faster accomplishments, a maximization of tempo, was not sanctioned by Auguste Comte. Intelligence, activity, and emotion should march ideally in step, three abreast, and any attempt of the intellectuals or the activists to be precocious only meant that they were breaking up the parade of order and progress. For Comte, untimely revolutions like the great French Revolution were in their consequences anarchic and retrogressive. The worst political catastrophes of the past were laid to a defect in the sense of timing; for the future the problem was of course less grave because fortunately there would be a High Priest of Humanity. Comte and his successors in the Positivist Church were the watchful ones, the leaders who would beat out the measure of progress with their sacerdotal batons, not too slow, not too fast, ever mindful of the optimum tempo for the emotive advance of mankind.

Comte abandoned an ideal of individual self-realization in favor of total absorption in humanity. In his last words to his disciples Saint-Simon had still insisted, "The essence of my life's work is to afford all members of society the greatest possible opportunity for the development of their faculties."[9] Men were to be joined in association and love, but the individual would not be lost; this was a Saint-Simonian pledge to prospective converts. With Auguste Comte, however, the Great Being became the time-bearing ocean in which all men would be engulfed. The individual found his true fulfillment only in suppressing his subjectivity. In the Positivist religion of total love there is a virtual loss of personality as we have known it in Western society.

In the end Auguste Comte's Great Being turned out to be even more cunning than Hegel's Reason. In the early stages of mankind the primitive had been forced to labor and to discover scientific facts that might alleviate the pains of his arduous tasks; finally, in the course of expanding his knowledge and his activity, he reached a point where both labor and science were transcended and free human nature could express itself directly in all-embracing love.

The times have changed radically since Auguste Comte was hounded into despair by the French academic community. As we shall see, the Jesuit paleontologist and Christian mystic, the late Teilhard de Chardin, and the English life-scientists J. B. S.

---

[9] *Notice historique,* in *Oeuvres de Saint-Simon et d'Enfantin,* I, 122.

Haldane and Julian Huxley, who have applied the Darwinian theory of evolution on a cosmic scale, are all fully aware of the affinities of their own doctrine with the Comtean vision of the Great Being—a vision that in his lifetime was treated with crushing contempt.

Thus by the mid-nineteenth century the idea of perfectibility had been profoundly altered. In the course of its history it had undergone many metamorphoses. With St. Augustine and the medieval religious thinkers it had been securely set in a Christian framework of spiritual perfection; by the seventeenth century linear progress in scientific knowledge had begun to be recognized, though it was not conceived as affecting the circular rhythm of power in the polity and was surely to be distinguished from the cycle of moral virtue. Toward the end of the eighteenth century occurred the crucial development. French thinkers came to see the possibility of transmuting scientific progress into moral and social progress and thus gradually identifying the two with each other, while still allowing for an autonomous cycle of artistic creativity. With the nineteenth century the various separate progressions were fused into one common conception of Progress encompassing all aspects of human creativity.

But this abstraction had barely been achieved when the whole idea of progress became problematic. Its acceleration had been accepted as a general moral ideal, but at that very moment the optimum practical methods for achieving it were opened to bloody dispute in the political arena. Advances in the diffusion of love, brotherhood, and humanity were more and more appreciated as the core of a new definition of progress, but the ways toward universal love became the subject of bitter strife and contention. While some came to preach the love of humanity, many others were armed to kill in its name.

6

Leaps into Free Consciousness:
Resonances from the German Academy

In 1821 a young American from Boston, the future historian George Bancroft, after successfully defending his doctoral thesis in a formal ceremony at Göttingen, made a tour of the German universities and finally arrived in Berlin. He was demonstrably bewildered. "I will become a follower of your sound empirical philosophy," he wrote back home to Professor Levi Frisbie, "rather than an adherer of Schelling and Hegel. To become acquainted with the systems of the German metaphysicians is indeed a most difficult and intricate undertaking." Of Hegel at the height of his fame, lecturing on the philosophy of history to large audiences, he wrote with downright abhorrence: "His delivery is abominable, his style execrable, his language to me almost unintelligible."[1]

The sentiments of George Bancroft were, with rare exceptions, widely shared by members of the Anglo-French community until relatively recent years. But even when they were reluctant to approach the thickets of idealist philosophy made impenetrable by the jargon of Fichte, Schelling, and Hegel, few doubted that a historical myth of great potency had been manufactured in the deep recesses of those German university towns. Though the idealist philosophy, "instead of going about on its head," was stood back on its feet again by Dr. Karl Marx

---

[1] Boston, Massachusetts Historical Society, Bancroft Papers, Mss: George Bancroft to Levi Frisbie, April 13, 1821.

as he boastfully proclaimed in a Postcript to the 1872 edition of *Das Kapital,* the Hegelian terminology and style never lost their grip on the Marxist doctrine. Wherever the doctrine went there went Hegel, and nowhere is this indissoluble bond more manifest than in contemporary France, where an important segment of the radical intellectuals have become latter-day Hegelians.

It is not my purpose to expound either the theory of Hegel or the theory of Marx in all their professorial and magisterial dogmatism, but rather to situate them in the context of this historical inquiry and to point up essential differences between the style and temper of the French and German schools of philosophical history, convinced as I am that their distinctions represent two divergent ways of viewing the historical world in modern times. Both belong to the general category progressive, but below this rubric they part.

I

Crossing the Rhine one is immediately struck by a different temper among the philosophers of history. The Germans were either pastors like Herder, sons of pastors like Lessing, or state university professors like Kant and Hegel. Germany was economically weak and politically divided, and despite the respectable positions occupied by the pastors and professors in their isolated principalities, they never presumed to exert direct influence on the external world of public affairs. At most they were educators. The philosophies of history they wrote were treatises that, by describing how the human species was fashioned in time, aimed to mold the inner beings of their students and their small literate public. Among the German pastors the militancy of a Luther had long since died. And in the university the distinction between the *vita activa* and the *vita contemplativa* was absolute. Kant had never left Königsberg; and Hegel insisted that the owl of Minerva, philosophy's grey-in-grey, only takes flight at dusk. Contemplation *after* the event. To the traditional German academic of that epoch, were he resurrected today, the contemporary activism of the American professoriat and its direct manipulation of power would not be the least astonishing aspect of our way of life. German philosophical discussions, even after the appearance of Marx, were remote from immediate political and social reality, and perhaps this very circumstance rendered them what Nietzsche would call *interessant*, in an interesting condition, pregnant with novel ideas. Political dormancy made the Germans more speculative and imaginative, less cut-and-dried, and often less sensible than their French counterparts.

The German style of philosophical history faithfully records the mood of these doctors of the inner life. In effect, the religious spirit of Luther—not his political activism—informs virtually all the works of the Germans. While the French wrote a secular history of man's expanding capacities and his outward achievements, the Germans composed a history of introverted man, a Protestant world history. The French systems were plainly sensationalist, under the influence of Locke and Condillac; the Germans remained profoundly theological, whether their authors shunned the church edifice as Kant did, or not. If a religious residue remained in the French outlook, it was a vision of man triumphing through good works. Cumulative progress was like a world treasury of merit to which the great scientific geniuses (the secular analogues of the saints) were all contributing their substance. The French are buoyantly optimistic, even if they are subject to moments of skepticism and doubt; while the Germans are profoundly pessimistic, even though they may write about perpetual peace, the ultimate fulfillment of man's nature, and the progressive conquest of Spirit. If the French school presents man's destiny as a utilitarianism temporalized or a history of pleasure and gratification, the Germans from Kant and Lessing down through Schelling and Hegel are writing a history of spiritual liberty accompanied by instinctual repression. Protestantism had taught them that illumination and knowledge of God were a long and arduous process requiring extraordinary exertions, soul-searching, and the effort of will. The German philosophers extended the history of individual God-seeking to the whole species. Even when they use words like *Fortgang* and *Fortschritt*, they do not at all mean what the French do by *progrès*.

The French philosophers of history concentrate on the novelties; they revel in the material conquests and in the new acquisitions. They take a Baconian delight in sheer accumulation and in the variety of objects. They enjoy what Montesquieu called *le bonheur de l'existence*. For the Germans, who made world history into a *Bildungsroman*, the education of the human race was no lark. There is throughout these writings a sense of the pain and anguish of growth. They were dealing with a refractory pupil who kicked against the pricks and learned only through punishment. Man refuses to quit his minority, lamented Kant, anticipating Freud. The Germans were always conscious of the bloody travail of history. While among most of the French the philosopher's eye was focused on the growing ease and the new rationality, the Germans, even the secularists among them, were weighed down by a sense of inborn evil. The baubles of French civilization they rejected with the moral righteousness of a Rousseau repudiating the arts and sciences.

II

For the Germans history had one meaning: the hard-won battle for consciousness, which is Hegel's Spirit, or the struggle for liberty, which even in Kant is not far removed from Luther's Christian liberty. Oracular dicta announce that world history is progress in the consciousness of freedom, that the ultimate purpose of the world is Spirit's consciousness of itself.

If viewed mechanically and only in his lectures of the 1820's, Hegel's history is a progressive realization of consciousness and freedom and spirit in the world through time; but it is hard to detect a triumphantly optimistic temper even in this work. Surely if one accepts the centrality of the problem of bad conscience in Hegel's historical world view, as the French philosopher Jean Wahl does,[2] it is rather difficult to be convinced by the final denouement of the historical drama. There is a lingering memory of the terrible contest of the individual and his collectives throughout time that is inherent in the very split (*Entzweiung*) of being. In new birth the pain and the torment predominate and become the essence of life. Hegel intones in melancholy vein: "Not only will Spirit experience from nature opposition and impediments, but it will often see its endeavors fail because of nature, and often it will succumb as a result of the intricate situations in which it has been falsely placed, either because of nature or because of itself."[3] The Hegelian Spirit wrestling with itself is always devoutly Protestant.

It is the state of contradiction that is creative, and for Hegel how miserably inadequate and superficial have been most past resolutions, especially the flat, French eighteenth-century one! Is not Hegel's world history a history of the forms and self-tortured grimaces of alienation throughout time, as well as the victory of Spirit? It was Hegel who first transformed the protagonist in Diderot's dialogue, *Rameau's Nephew*, into the symbol of the totally alienated man, when it was published in a German translation by Goethe even before it appeared in

---

[2] Jean André Wahl, *Le Malheur de la conscience dans la philosophie de Hegel* (Paris, 1929).
[3] Georg Wilhelm Friedrich Hegel, *Vorlesungen über die Philosophie der Geschichte* (Stuttgart, 1961), p. 130.

French. In a few passages of the *Phenomenology of Spirit* on the new industrial order and the psychological character of the alienated human relationships it was establishing, Hegel presaged Marx's trenchant critique.

When history was embodied in a world-historical figure like Caesar or Napoleon, he trampled underfoot many a moral flower, because individuals had to be sacrificed to the course of Spirit. For Hegel the fashioning of Spirit came to entail a maiming loss as well as a gain, as it had in Herder's first essay on philosophical history. While hailing the triumph of the Idea and the Protestant German state in which it found its most complete expression, the final resolution of the conflict between objectivity and subjectivity, Hegel takes more than a yearning look backward to the Greek ideal of his youth; there is in him a longing for the image of spontaneous, beautiful Hellas which he had once shared with his friend, the poet Friedrich Hölderlin. No German of the nineteenth century was ever completely consoled for the death of the youth of mankind that was Greece. History transcends itself; Absolute Spirit is victorious; but what a terrible price has to be paid by sensate man!

There had of course been a brief romantic moment in the earliest beginnings of this German nineteeth-century philosophy when it had a joyous expansiveness very different from the temper of the mature Hegel, Professor at Berlin. Three of the greatest geniuses of modern times composed the original pronouncement of German idealism when they were students together at Tübingen. The manuscript is in Hegel's hand, its contents are believed to have been drafted by Schelling, and its poetic spirit is Hölderlin's. Kant's excessively rationalist view of ethical man, as they understood it, had left them with a feeling of dissatisfaction. They joined in a commitment to the idea of progression, but progression of another order than Kant's: they dreamed of mankind's leap in one great bound into a new stage of consciousness. Their filiation was with

Schiller's ideal in the *Aesthetic Letters* and Lessing's freemasonic fantasies, and they rejected Kant's philosophy for its absorption in the legal and external political constraints that history systematically imposed on instinctual man.

Gone were the Kantian doubts about progress and the backings and fillings of Herder. These young poet-philosophers saluted the coming into being of a new man, spontaneously aesthetic and harmonious. They hoped to deliver reason from the bonds of criticism, which had destroyed all feeling, above all religious feeling, and to achieve a new synthesis of the rational and the mythological, the abstract and the concrete, as the third and highest stage of the human psyche. To rescue mythic consciousness from the clutch of Hamann's religiosity and reason from the limitations of Kant's critical analysis was the earnest intent of their pact. They no longer debated progress, as had the eighteenth-century Germans; they worshiped it. But it was progress in freedom conceived as the Platonic idea of the beautiful. "The philosophy of spirit is an aesthetic philosophy," they proclaimed.[4] Their idealist utopia was of a psychic rather than a social order, but it had none of the chill of Absolute Spirit. Alas, the young poet Hölderlin went mad, and the two philosophers Schelling and Hegel grew older. Their formal allegiance to the progress of Spirit may have remained the same; its style and mood surely changed. It lost its poetic universality and became parochial; it lost its enthusiasm for the future and became nostalgic.

III

Among the French, philosophical history was cosmopolitan and on the whole egalitarian. Despite their unshakable conviction that they were in the vanguard of the historical process and that Paris was the mount from which the new gospel was to be

---

[4] *Das Älteste Systemprogramm des deutschen Idealismus* (fragment), in Friedrich Hölderlin, *Sämtliche Werke,* 3d edition (Berlin, 1943), III, 623.

delivered, the bounty of civilization was universally communicable to all races and peoples who were willing to assimilate it and become a part of progressive history. Not so the Germans. It is with some sense of shock that in an early essay we read Kant's harsh dismissal of the black race as incapable of reason —passages, by the way, that are omitted from the compendia gathered by his devoted admirers.[5] To Hegel meaningful historical activity was the destiny only of an infinitesimal body of the elect among the nations. He was more selective than the most hard-bitten Calvinist. The actual living experience of most peoples was doomed to oblivion, insofar as the world history of the Idea was concerned. Hegel wrote at the end of the *Philosophy of Right*: "Each of its stages is the presence of a necessary moment in the Idea of the world mind, and that moment attains its absolute right in that stage. The nation whose life embodies this moment secures its good fortune and fame, and its deeds are brought to fruition."[6] But at any given moment there is only one embodiment in one particular world-historical nation; events in all other nations at that moment of Idea are empty, devoid of meaning. All prehistory (in his definition life before the consolidated state) is without content. Hegel's world history is really confined to a few rare periods of perfection in a succession of national cultures. There are chosen moments in four or five chosen cultures. For the rest, there is nothing but inchoate barbarism or else decay.

Seen through the eyes of the Germans, history is a holocaust. For Schelling, it is a tragic spectacle performed on the mournful stage of the world. Hegel's Absolute Spirit has traveled in stages from China to Germany, embodying itself temporarily

---

[5] Immanuel Kant, "Observations on the Feeling of the Beautiful and Sublime," in *Essays and Treatises*, II (1799), 74: "The blacks are remarkably vain, but in a negro manner, and so loquacious, that they must absolutely be separated by the cogent and conclusive argument of caning."

[6] Hegel, *Philosophy of Right*, translated and with notes by T. M. Knox (Oxford, 1942), p. 217.

in one world-historical state after another, nourishing itself on one national genius after another. Once a nation had passed its zenith, Spirit moved on to the next in order, leaving the now soulless people to drag itself on through years of uncreative nullity, busied with politics and perhaps war, with a senile repetition of itself, until it finally died in the body, having long since been dead in spirit. If Hegel's Spirit triumphs it triumphs amid the death of cultures.

In Hegel's *Philosophy of Right* the dread exclusiveness of the Idea is pronounced with a thunderous crash befitting a *Weltgericht,* a world court of judgment, handing down its verdict: "The nation to which is ascribed a moment of the Idea in the form of a natural principle is entrusted with giving complete effect to it in the advance of the self-developing self-consciousness of the world mind. This nation is dominant in world history during this one epoch, and it is only once that it can make its hour strike. In contrast with this its absolute right of being the vehicle of this present stage in the world mind's development, the minds of the other nations are without rights, and they, along with those whose hour has struck already, count no longer in world history."

What happens when a nation has passed its prime and has been abandoned by World Spirit? "Perhaps it loses its autonomy, or it may still exist, or drag out its existence, as a particular state or a group of states and involve itself without rhyme or reason in manifold enterprises at home and battles abroad."[7] The debris of history, the ash-heap of history—a Marxist concept the Russians have adopted to depict the losers in the struggle—is profoundly Hegelian. There are some of us for whom history is a natural right, for whom even lost causes may have a most glorious history. Not so with Hegel's Spirit.

During each incarnation of Spirit, a culture went through

[7] *Ibid.,* pp. 217–18.

the organic cycle from birth to death, its destruction coming about from an antithetic element within it. And thus Hegelian philosophy of history has the individual culture cycle, the unilinear triumphant world spirit, and the dialectic between the genius of one cultural incarnation and its successor. The individual freedom of the Greek soul, destroyed by the anarchic subjectivity of the city-states in suicidal internecine warfare, is followed by the universality and slavery of the Roman. The Greek cyclical experience is the model for all embodiments of Spirit.

Sometimes Hegel's shape of philosophical history is joined to strange theories with a dark future. It is one thing to describe these leaps of Spirit from culture to culture; and it all sounds so wondrously abstract and rational, as Spirit moves from China through Greece and Rome to its German embodiment. But why is this historical climax in Germandom and why not in the Latin peoples? The answer is in the end racial purity, blood—a word that is sometimes forgotten by latter-day Hegelians. The Latin nations were formed by an admixture of Latin and German blood, according to Hegel. And because of this miscegenation, they are not an appropriate, fitting abode for the highest form of Spirit. How readily Absolute Spirit can backslide to a *Blut und Boden* theory!

Here Hegel closely approaches Herder, though he rarely mentions him. Herder too identified creativity with *Volk* purity. In describing world-history the Germans regard the moments of intermingling as the ugly ones, for they give birth to half-breeds. In virtually all philosophical history those who concentrate exclusively on the abstraction of a nation or a culture or a civilization or a race as the organic historical unit of discourse have a fatal tendency to regard any intermixture as poisoning, corrupting, and diluting. The number of such theories is legion: in Gobineau's doctrine racial contamination later became the historical event that directly determined decay and destruction. Hegel rejected the Latin nations, not only because they failed to achieve "innerness," but because they were mongrel and polluted.

Perhaps the character of this German form of philosophical history is again best brought out by contrast with the sensationalist or arithmetic progressivism of the Turgot-Condorcet type. They are opposites. In the French system a closed or isolated culture is in continuous peril of stultification; the rut of sameness is mortal. The multiplication of communications, the creation of new relationships is the key to new perceptions, hence to new ideas. Endless novelty invites new impressions and discoveries. The French look upon cross-fertilization as the highest good, productive of science, technology, and ultimately moral perfectibility. The Germans, on the other hand, tend to view cross-fertilization as destructive of values, style, identity, structure, growth. The intrusion from the outside is alien, unnatural, inimical to form and cohesiveness. German race theories did not need to await the new biology; they had already acquired philosophical roots in the conceptualization of culture itself in Herder and Hegel.

The degree to which the nineteenth-century progressivists of the German idealist persuasion incorporated cyclical theory merits at least passing notice. I have had my times with mathematicians, as I asked for a graphic term to describe the Hegelian system, at once cyclical and progressive. And the adjectives I got, sinusoidal and cycloid, are probably no better than Hegel deserves. Nineteenth-century writers preferred the analogy to a spiral. In this respect Hegel's idea of the progress of Spirit offers merely one solution to the problem that Herder had never resolved, of how some connexities are established between the isolated culture cycles. And the progressive shape of this theory should not be stressed to the neglect of the circular element. When Spirit rests for a while in Greece, for example, during the course of its four kangaroo leaps into absolute self-realization, it does in fact experience a total cycle from birth to death. Though Spirit may be progressive, the actual content of history experienced by men, lived by human beings within any one culture, remains cyclical. They have to suffer long years of decline and disintegration and their moral characters are stamped with the mark of decay.

In the French philosophies of history, men obtain the society that they seek, above all when they obey the dictates of an enlightened utilitarianism. For Hegel the creation of a free society of law and order is achieved in despite of the human passions which are its constituent elements. Like the building materials that go into the construction of a house, one of his favorite similes, they each have their own natures and resistances and yet somehow the house is built. There is a disjunction between human will and its realization, between what men desire passionately and what history will grant. History is therefore unpredictable. Though it is a function of human activity it transcends this activity and becomes the field of combat where Spirit, not man, lays down the rules of destiny.

Since the French saw man as endlessly malleable and his reason easily amenable to novelty, a long hiatus between the discovery of a new truth and its implementation in history was not inherently necessary. The speed of change depended on the wills of men, which could be rationally organized for maximum effectiveness; progress could be accelerated through reform. The French *philosophes* from Turgot down, with their geometric pattern of enlightenment—blocks of darkness that presented danger and of light that in time would penetrate the black—expected this conversion of superstition to scientism to take place as painlessly and as fast as possible. Even Auguste

Comte, the Frenchman most committed to a stadial theory, nevertheless argued in the *Positive Polity* that the contemporary savage world could rapidly advance from fetishism to scientism (naturally under the appropriate tutelage of Parisians), skipping the intermediate stages through which Western Europe had passed because the universal progressist model had already been set.

Beginning with Herder, German philosophical history was bound to a slow genetic sense of time. Benign transformations in national genius had sometimes taken place through the penetration of its hard core, but only with the passage of ages. For each being, each *Volk*, for mankind itself, there was an ordained time-span of growth and decay, and there was no way that organized wills could affect this biological life-process. In Hegel, even World Spirit was obliged to drag itself laboriously through cycle after cycle, and there was nothing which could have accelerated or delayed its tragic trek. From genetic time there was no appeal. To interfere in a nation's natural historical development meant to destroy its inner being. The effects of political reform were highly dubious. The promulgation of constitutions and similar social innovations was futile unless there were prior spiritual transformation of the soul of the people. This required time and was totally dependent upon the stage of the culture cycle. Hegel as a young student had saluted the French Revolution as the triumph of Reason. Professor Hegel in his lectures on the philosophy of history three decades later brushed it aside as abortive, meaningless for World Spirit, because it had not been preceded by a long religious reformation such as Protestantism, the unique good fortune of Germandom.

French philosophy of history deals with events and actions; German, with the soul. Though both use a terminology that betrays a common Christian origin, the French wrote a history of the achievements of the mind and humanity (to amend Condorcet), the Germans a history of Spirit itself, for which men and their deeds are only vessels. Perhaps in their contrasting sense of historical time do we finally perceive the most fundamental difference between the French and the German schools —French progress is continuous and subject to rapid change, German is discontinuous in its leaps and beyond human will to alter. I would even hazard the reflection that sciences of man, down to our own day, called upon to depict process in time— whether economic growth or child development—find themselves forced to choose between these two modes developed by French and German philosophical history.

IV

Introduced against this intellectual background of the two classical systems of France and Germany, so alike in their acceptance of the common nineteenth-century conception of progress and yet so profoundly different in style, temper, and method, the Rhinelander Dr. Karl Marx appears as a major syncretic figure. Educated in the German university system in the decade after Hegel's death, when Hegelianism dominated the intellectual atmosphere, he took his degree at the University of Jena in 1841 with a Latin dissertation on the difference between the Democritan and the Epicurean philosophies of nature. Within a few years, he found himself an expatriate in France, caught up in the welter of Parisian conspiratorial circles and militant strike movements. There he was exposed to the writings of the French philosophers of history and utopian thinkers—Saint-Simon, Fourier, and the Saint-Simonians—who had died or had passed out of their creative period at about the same time as Hegel succumbed to the cholera in 1831. Thus two souls strove for mastery in Marx's turbulent breast and yielded a hybrid philosophy of history that is of the tree of true knowledge to some and of a deadly poison to others. Perhaps in the last analysis it depends on the dosage.

From the French Marx inherited his scientism, his belief in the directing force of technological innovation in the historical process, his simple utilitarianism, his acceptance of the desires of the flesh and the extrovert works of men as absolute good, his commitment to materialism in the sense that matter counts and that the different ways of working, eating, and fulfilling creature needs are a respectworthy subject of historical inquiry, perhaps its central thread. While Hegel had taught that men were distinguished from one another only in spirit, Marx in working-class Paris of the 1840's learned to appreciate the history of labor, of class struggle, of the changing organization of production in different epochs, and the passion of the quest for sensate happiness among those who lived in squalor. What Marx did to Hegel, posthumously to be sure, was to point out a fact that Hegel with his extraordinary feeling for reality had probably sensed but which he never uttered in a straightforward manner: that a harmony of subjective ego-desire and objective power had not in practice been achieved by the vast number of human beings in the world, even if it had been by a few Berlin professors in the Prussian *Rechtstaat*. And Marx then went on to insist that one ought to do something about it. "Philosophers have hitherto merely interpreted the world variously," he wrote in his *Theses on Feuerbach* in 1845. "The issue is to change it."[8]

But this does not mean that Marx had ever sloughed off his Hegelian skin. His view of history is fundamentally in the German tradition, sharply and catastrophically discontinuous. History moves in revolutionary jumps through a series of orga-

[8] Karl Marx, "Marx über Feuerbach," in *Gesamtausgabe*, Part I, 5 (Berlin, 1932), 535.

nized systems of production relations, identifiable forms of economic life, units that can be studied as complete self-sufficient entities with a substructure and a superstructure. They are not static unified bodies because the world-historical process is progressive, not peaceful bodies because class war is perennial, but systems that bear lasting names. In the *Critique of Political Economy* of 1859 the stages of what he called man's prehistory —for him true human history would only dawn with communism—are four in number, and they describe progressive periods in the economic evolution of all societies in the world. Marx's four modes of production replaced Hegel's four world-historical cultures, as these had once ousted Daniel's four world monarchies. Marx described these stages or modes at various times as oriental or patriarchal; antique or slave; feudal or serf; capitalist or bourgeois. All of these systems have been incomplete and antagonistic forms of society within which class conflict has raged unabated. The process is dialectical, revolutionary not gradualist. There are sudden spurts of violence when the slowly maturing new forces, which have long been smothered by old ruling classes, suddenly burst forth to seize power.

Historical periodization in Marx as in Hegel has real meaning: it has sharp boundaries. If his conception of social forces is essentially scientific, organizational, and technological in the French manner, the life-cycle of an economic system and its demise is depicted by Marx with the same pathos that Hegel had once lavished on the death of cultures. In the *Communist Manifesto* Marx composed passages of high dramatic intensity describing the grandeur of capitalism and its triumphs that would do any nineteenth-century liberal economist proud. But Marx was building up his capitalist system into a hero out of Shakespearean tragedy (of which he had a deep appreciation) only in order to destroy him.

As for the existential content of the happiness achieved at the end of the prehistoric process, to preserve Marx's private nomenclature, it amalgamates both German and French elements. Each of the four leaps represents a massive acquisition of freedom and consciousness by a new, previously exploited and suppressed social class. Through history slaves, serfs, workers, and petty bourgeois had each in their turn been manipulated by other classes, but in the final struggle all mankind would achieve a liberty that had once been granted piecemeal to different segments of society. While Hegel remained tragically ambiguous about the ultimate human condition even after the triumph of Spirit, Marx was on the whole more in the optimist commonsensical tradition of English and French utopians. For him alienation was primarily an economic concept dealing with human labor, the pouring of man's being into a machine, which came to lord it over him like a fetish god, his own creation turned into his master. Marx's concept of alienation only rarely has the overtones that the idea has acquired in contemporary psychological and literary fashion.

Philosophical and artistic creations were for Marx reflections of economic and social systems, even as for Hegel they were mirrors of a particular moment in the history of spirit. Marx believed that in the end of the days this creative consciousness would no longer be false, that is, merely expressive of the taste of a specific ruling class. It would cease to be the voice of partial slavery and become totally free and actual. If in Hegel the abstract in art would be the inevitable consequence of the triumph of Absolute Spirit—a brilliant prophecy—in Marx free consciousness probably spelt the end of philosophy. Since all past philosophy had been determined by the false consciousness of class interest, when men had finally achieved true consciousness in a classless society there would be nothing to philosophize about. In this respect the poverty of philosophy in the Soviet world is a faithful illustration of Marxist doctrine.

For Hegel the great moment of art was gone forever because the culture of ancient Hellas had passed. Never again would it be possible to achieve that perfect union of free spirit with the objective corporeal world which was the glory of Greece. Marx was possessed by the same nostalgia for ancient Greece as the rest of the Germans, but his version of the future of art is somewhat different. While man cannot become like a child again he is not prevented from enjoying a child's naïveté or from aspiring to the naïve truth of a child on a higher level. The art of Greece can therefore continue to exert its eternal fascination upon us even though it reflects the social infancy of mankind. A furtive glimpse at an Aphrodite or an Apollo will be allowable in the future society despite the fact that they were expressions of a slave society, unworthy of a modern free man.

In his views on the history of work and the future of the state Marx was far closer to the French than to the Germans. Consciousness as a historical concept was too abstract a notion for the French philosopher-historians, with the exception of Comte; but the concrete reality of labor and power and desire was their common coin, and in this realm Marx for the most part reflected their school rather than the German.

In a famous letter, the *Critique of the Gotha Programme* (1875), which has had an enduring influence on communist thought, Marx wrote of the highest phase of future communist society, the goal of history: "After the enslaving subordination of individuals to the division of labor has disappeared, and with it the contradiction between intellectual and physical work; after labor has become not only a means for life, but itself the prime necessity of living; after the forces of production have grown, along with the many-sided development of the individual, and all the wellsprings of communal riches flow more plentifully—only then can the narrow, bourgeois horizon of rights be completely transcended, and society inscribe on its

banners: from each according to his abilities, to each according
to his needs!"[9] This oft-quoted formulation of the communist
ideal, which Khrushchev would repeat at party congresses like
an ancient litany, is clearly a syncretism of ideas and phrases
garnered from the French, particularly from the Saint-Simonians and the Fourierists. Of course, Marx's historical analysis
of "needs," intimately related to the Hegelian problem of
alienation, is a more complex conceptualization, in many ways
far more subtle philosophically than anything the Frenchmen
propounded. Nonetheless, all of them were aiming their arrows
in the same direction. Marx's "self-actualization of the individual,"[10] Saint-Simon's "development of faculties," and Fourier's
plea for the "burgeoning of instinct," moral ideals with a long
past history, in our time have come to be articulate, almost universal demands. While need still retains a simple alimentary
content for starving hundreds of millions, the more expansive
definition of need first essayed by the French utopians and by
Marx follows fast upon the appeasement of hunger and is no
longer considered extravagant, as it was in the nineteenth century.

However much Marx differed from the French philosophers
in analyzing the historical process itself, there was agreement
between them that the new society emerging from the last conflict of systems or classes would witness the twilight of power
and the cessation of conflicts among men. Both saw power and
aggressiveness not as ineradicable characteristics of man but as
transient historical manifestations generated by previous, im-
perfect social systems and destined to perish with them. Their
optimism was a corollary to their analysis of the classes desig-

[9] Marx, *Kritik des Gothaer Programms* (Berlin, 1946), p. 21; originally a postscript
in a letter to Bracke, May 5, 1875, it was first printed in *Neue Zeit* in 1891.
[10] The phrase "Selbstverwirklichung des Individuums" occurs in Marx's manuscripts
of the 1850's that have come to be known as *Grundrisse der Kritik der Politischen
Ökonomie (Rohentwurf) 1857–1858* (Berlin, 1953), p. 505.

nated as the agents of the last revolution. The proletarians were in their nature men who worked, not men who exploited, hence by definition they could not engineer a proletarian revolution and thereafter exploit others. It would be contrary to their nature to become intoxicated with power. The simplicity with which socialist theory both of the Marxist and French variety turned its head away from the cruel realities of the power drive in man was perhaps the great blind spot of their outlook.

v

Leading ideas from these French and German schools of philosophical history have been transmitted to twentieth-century thinkers and have seeped into popular ideologies. It would be supererogatory on my part to offer examples of the endurance of the French model of philosophical history in our time. It is the sea around us. From historical doctrine it has in our society become official dogma. The German style, too, has persisted, perhaps most of all in the writings of Protestant theologians educated in the German tradition. Even in Spengler, despite some of his disparaging references to the philosophies of history of Herder, Kant, and Hegel in the introduction to *The Decline of the West* and his different conception of historical morphology, one can still discern the same pervasive tragic spirit, the same genetic sense of time, and the same basic concept of cultural exhaustion.

By the Second World War, however, I must admit that the national character of these two types of philosophical history no longer held as firmly as it used to. In a strange spiritual transvestism, the two attitudes represented by the French and the Germans have sometimes switched sides. The French have recently taken Hegel to their bosoms. Simone de Beauvoir reports somewhere that she found herself reading him in the Bibliothèque Nationale the day the Germans entered Paris—

a double conquest. Conversely, it would appear that the Germans have had enough of *Innerlichkeit*. The break with their philosophical tradition is all but complete, and the new Germany has risen out of the ashes to a material acquisitiveness and practicality, to a belief in sensate progress that has left Hegel's Spirit far behind—and it may be to the good.

As for Marxism, to the extent that it became a revolutionary action program its main influence was probably in the old-time French activist spirit rather than the German contemplative one. Nevertheless, one might hazard the reflection that some measure of the discontinuous nature of contemporary Soviet policy, its sudden shifts which bewilder us when embodied in specific political actions, may in part be imputed to its long immersion in the idea of historical discontinuity that characterized the German school of philosophical history in its formative period. This is not meant as a day-to-day working clue to communist policy, which for the most part had better be explained in terms of *Realpolitik*, but it does perhaps help to identify the philosophical spirit in which that policy is drafted.

We have, I hope, long since learned that one does not have to be a philosopher to be influenced by philosophy. Its effect is not readily visible, but it can be all the more enduring for its subtlety. In closing I should like to recall what Saint-Simon once said about the penetration of intellectual influences, because it holds for these nineteenth-century resonances from the German academy, Hegel and Marx, as well as for the French doctrinaires of perfectibility. "General ideas," he reflected, "may be compared to musk. One does not have to see it or touch it in order to sense its odor."[11]

---

[11] Henri de Saint-Simon, *Introduction aux travaux scientifiques du xixe siècle* (1807), in *Oeuvres choisies,* I, 68n.

7
An Uneasy Consensus:
The Twentieth-Century Prospect

THE TWENTIETH-CENTURY efflorescence of philosophies of history has spawned more works in four decades than have all previous ages of man combined. The literature has become so voluminous that no sun rises in the East but to greet the birth of a new philosophy of history or the refutation of an old one. Confronted by the hundreds of volumes on philosophical history that have poured forth from the printing presses of the world in our time, one stands in amazement at this rebirth of an intellectual problem that positivistic historians of the second half of the nineteenth century would have assured you was dead and gone forever. Today, it serves no purpose to join Wilhelm Dilthey, Benedetto Croce, and a host of good historical craftsmen in mockery, insisting that a philosophy of history is a contradiction in terms, that it cannot possibly exist. To assure yourself of its reality, simply stub your toe with a Johnsonian gesture on the twelve volumes of Arnold Toynbee, the two of Oswald Spengler, the four of Pitirim Sorokin, Eric Voegelin's hexology, the repetitive corpus of Nicolas Berdyaev and of Reinhold Niebuhr, even the more modest works of Father d'Arcy, Christopher Dawson, Alfred Weber, and Karl Jaspers, not to speak of the English theorists of evolution and of Teilhard de Chardin, of the latter-day representatives of the idea of material and scientific progress, and of a variety of contemporary Marxists.

The title of this lecture might raise a suspicion that the au-

thor has himself finally succumbed to the *morbus philosophistoricus* and means to contribute his mite to the deluge. Some
immediate reassurance is therefore in order. I come before you
to bear witness to the flood, not to swell it.

My position with respect to these philosophies of history is
analogous to that of a modern mythographer of the psychological persuasion who may concede that the myths are false
in a commonsensical way, but who has to confess that an important part of him still lives in a mythopoeic world. The urge
to place himself in a total time sequence—the real impetus to
philosophical history—seems to have possessed Western man
for more than two thousand years; and it is probably stronger
in our culture than in most others we know. This is the empirical point from which I start. I do not know whether the need
will survive the twentieth century, but the remarkable lon-
gevity of the main themes of philosophical history leads me
to doubt whether they will be destroyed by mere criticism. Individuals are continually reorienting themselves to the historical order of their lives, rewriting their autobiographies and
making secret predictions to themselves, condemning themselves to an imminent death, foretelling a glorious future of
delights, philosophically facing a decline into senility. Similarly, our societies have from time to time constructed new pic-
tures of the total meaning of historical existence, and these have
almost always included predictions of things to come as well as
a reduction of the whole of the past to an order. These efforts
are what I call philosophies of history. Self-conscious epochs
have had a way of telling their age. They have boisterously
proclaimed the fact that they feel young and vigorous and believe themselves to be the sons of a new birth; or they have
not concealed from themselves the painful truth that they are
weighed down with the burden of their years, often predicting,
with amazing accuracy, their impending doom. They have of
course not always been right.

I

At first glance the present-day agglomeration of literature on philosophical history appears to be a vast inchoate mass, but if you stare at it long enough and hard enough, it has a way of dividing itself up into a few distinct segments. It is my purpose to serve you as both a witness and a dragoman, and if my groupings discontent you, as well they may, I would ask you simply to accept them as a mid-twentieth-century version of Dilthey's famous dream.

In the rough, one great divide still separates off those who infuse new meaning into the idea of progression from those who reject it as a blind fiction and instead seek to fashion the mountains of historical data that have accumulated in recent centuries into a circular theory, more sophisticated than the ancient one but in the same mold.

In their turn the progressists can be subdivided into at least three types: first, those who are loyally bound to the French concept of perfectibility in any one of its late eighteenth- or nineteenth-century forms; second, a new school of philosophical life-scientists writing cosmic history; and last, the contemporary Marxists. If the current proponents of the French idea of perfectibility are no longer as buoyantly confident as nineteenth-century progressists once were, the content of their ideas has remained in many respects unaltered, and their position will be taken for granted in this lecture.

We should perhaps distinguish a fourth type of progressist, though I wonder whether they do not warrant a special category altogether. The group I refer to are the modern Christian theologians of history who severely restrict themselves to spiritual progression, and who have become, as St. Augustine once was, among the most zealous denigrators of the idea of earthly progress.

Proceeding from the highest to the lowest I shall begin with this last group, who are responsible for the modern rebirth of the theology of history, and then turn to the more mundane doctrines. The theologians are after all heirs to one of the oldest philosophies of history. With the possible exception of the eighteenth-century materialists and Karl Marx, none of the major systems of the past ever divested itself completely of a providential cast. Vico still considered his *New Science* a rational civil theology of Divine Providence, and Hegel called his system a theodicy, a justification of God. The subject has always been so imbued with religious emotion that many modern readers have taken deep drafts of the philosophy of history in order to immerse themselves in a quasi-religious experience. Thomas Churchill, an eighteenth-century English translator of both Herder and Condorcet, testified to the religious inspiration he derived from the philosophy of history in language quite reminiscent of Freud's description of the religious "oceanic feeling."

In the twentieth century, religious thinkers of the three major Christian Churches, Catholic, Protestant, and Greek Orthodox, have felt it incumbent upon them to re-enter this field of inquiry with the avowed and deliberate purpose of rescuing the holy grail of the philosophy of history from the hands of the heathens and the secularizers of the providential design. They have addressed themselves to the arrogant presumption of nineteenth-century system-makers that there can be a worldly resolution to the problems of human history, with Christian eschatology either omitted or pushed into the background. The goal and purpose of history lies beyond our terrestrial sphere.

The religious thinkers have a common commitment to Christianity as a historical but transcendent religion that is now determined and probably was determined in the mind of God before time. Moreover, universal history has an axis that is in the middle of the historical process—the breakthrough of the divine into the world in the person of Christ. The *Kairos* in Paul Tillich's sense establishes an absolute measure of judgment for the future in the past; and thereby contemporary Christian philosophy of history is distinguished, without the possibility of a conciliation, from all the modern secular systems for whom the process was either ethically meaningless in its circularity or directed toward a worldly goal that is set in the future.[1]

Beyond this point unanimity among the Christian philosophers of history begins to vanish, and despite the ecumenical tendencies of our times, differences appear among the three sectarian positions that have deep roots in their theologies. Of late the Catholic view is perhaps less engaged in the contest against the illusions of progress than most Protestant theologians, a complete reversal of historical positions since the nineteenth century. Protestant theology of history is more self-consciously Augustinian, more emphatic on the role of sin and on the dangers of an intrusion of the daemonic into the world, insisting upon the struggle for Christian morality as a duty in the midst of the ambiguities of history, but none too sanguine about the temporal outcome. The Greek Orthodox in its prerevolutionary Russian form is far more apocalyptic than either the Protestant or the Catholic.

When in 1955 Pope Pius XII delivered an address in the Vatican before the assembled members of the International Historical Congress, he was at some pains to reject the idea

---

[1] "The center of history is the place where the meaning-giving principle of history is seen.... The claim of every other point in history to be a center, to be capable of giving meaning to history, is consistently denied.... Now, this is the claim which in Christianity is expressed in the idea of Christ." Paul Tillich, *The Interpretation of History*, translated by N. A. Rasetzki and E. L. Talmey (New York, 1936), pp. 250, 251.

that the thirteenth was the great Catholic century from which there had been a steady regression into heresy, pagan materialism, and modernism. This had been the argument of traditionalist French Catholic philosophers of the romantic reaction, de Bonald and de Maistre, in combat with the rationalism and scientism of the French revolutionary idea of progress; their views have now been abandoned as too restrictive a frame for Catholic history. The encyclicals of Pope John XXIII were almost Saint-Simonian in their commitment to material, social, and moral progress, and a traditionalist might seek in vain for the mention of sin in *Pacem in Terris*. The general position of the twentieth-century Catholic Church seems to eschew any specific philosophy of history and to allow a wide spectrum of divergent beliefs and opinions to coexist beneath its canopy. The writings of Christopher Dawson are perhaps characteristic of an outlook that has moved radically away from the pompous, dogmatic assertion of intimate knowledge of God's way in the world as propounded by a Bossuet or by the darker side of the nineteenth-century Catholic reaction. Christopher Dawson rejects both a totally idealist interpretive key to history, which would become exclusively absorbed in religion or the idea, and a thoroughly materialist one that finds motive drives only in the organization of power.

Dawson appreciates cultures and civilizations, including the primitive, primarily as expressions of man's religious creativity, but since the physical and the spiritual are consubstantial in man and there can be no great religious manifestation without a materialist power as an underpinning, the noblest religious discoveries of the highest cultures are ultimately bound to dissolve in corruption and decay. Therefore cycles of civilization are probably inevitable. Whenever the material nature of a culture permeates the whole and drives out its spiritual nature, death must follow. This is the heart of his attack on the absolute worth of material technological progress in the modern world. "The events of the last few years," he said in the Gifford Lectures of 1947, "portend either the end of human history or a turning point in it. They have warned us in letters of fire that our civilization has been tried in the balance and found wanting—that there is an absolute limit to the progress that can be achieved by the perfectionment of scientific techniques detached from spiritual aims and moral values."[2] But unlike Spengler, he never conceives of the historical discontinuities between cultures as complete. On the contrary, at the time when dying cultures and new conquering cultures intermingle, harmonies of human existence are established, and these are among the great creative moments in the history of world civilization. Dawson emerges as the defender of syncretism against Germanic ideologies of social and cultural purity which despised amalgamations, and this allows him moreover to preserve the unity of world history in the age-old Christian manner.

Assimilation of the Joachimite heresy with its emphasis on a golden age in this world had brought liberal Protestantism—under Enlightenment influence—dangerously close to identification with the secular idea of progress. The new Protestant theology of history of the twentieth century has broken with this tradition and fights what it conceives to be the misguided, facile optimism of both Christian and secular liberalism, which hides the moral taint inherent in all reformist and meliorist movements. Christian faith is perverted, warns Reinhold Niebuhr, if it lends itself to the expectation of the kingdom of the righteous in this world. Such utopian hope hides the fact that "corruptions of the meaning of life are bound to appear on every level of history, so long as human freedom is real freedom and therefore contains the possibility of evil."[3] An attack-

[2] Christopher Henry Dawson, *Religion and Culture* (London, 1948), p. 215.
[3] Reinhold Niebuhr, *Faith and History: A Comparison of Christian and Modern Views of History* (New York, 1949), p. 211.

ing revolutionary force that destroys an old order gone rotten is merely the scourge of God performing a divine mission. But alas the scourges are not content to remain instruments of Providence; they soon claim god-like qualities. In their arrogance they set themselves up as idols in the place of the defeated power and before long reveal their own wedlock with evil, the destiny of all worldly power. Since there can be no disinterested executors of judgment in history there can never be a progressive abolition of evil, as the Enlightenment had pretended.[4]

Niebuhr seems so overwhelmed by the evil imbedded in any new manifestation of power, in its idolatrous self-esteem, that he appears to strip the culture itself of all worth. He is terrified by liberal Protestantism's identification of religion with progressive civilization. "At their worst, sectarian Christianity, liberal Christianity, and modern secular liberalism have all become united in the errors and sentimentalities of a soft utopianism, which manages to evade the tragic realities of life and to obscure the moral ambiguity in all political positions. These evasions are achieved by hoping for a progressive alteration of the character of human history."[5] Niebuhr's God is totally hidden and his religion is almost Jansenist in withholding merit from anything in this world, in refusing a Christian embrace. The dying power is corroded with evil and sin and it is just that it perish. The new secular Messianism that promises to bring heaven on earth is even worse because it is more vigorous, younger, and more arrogant. Civilizations at best are transitory historical harmonies, and though there are moments when Niebuhr describes them as affording partial views of Agape, Christian love, he is markedly less moved by this tiny bit of truth discernible in a culture than he is by its false pretension to being total truth.

The Greek Orthodox view represented by Nicolas Berdyaev,

---

[4] *Ibid.*, pp. 227–28.
[5] *Ibid.*, p. 208.

whose major work was delivered as lectures in Russia in the early years of the Revolution before his exile, is far more mystical than either contemporary Catholic or Protestant thought. Great historical events—particularly revolutions—symbolize God's judgment in history. The redemption will be a redemption *from* history. The whole vision is transcendent and there are no glib compromises with the efficient causes of the positivistic historians. Sin, crime, punishment, and forgiveness are the primary historical categories, and history in its innermost meaning remains a commentary on the Apocalypse. Like Dawson, Berdyaev accepts the inevitability of the culture cycle, denigrating Spengler's originality *en passant*, turning to the many Russian nineteenth-century prophets of the doom of the materialist, progressist, and mechanistic West as his source, perhaps not realizing how dependent they in their turn had been on earlier German cyclical theorists. The death of a civilization or a political regime is, however, primarily a religious phenomenon for Berdyaev, the visitation of a divine punishment. "Revolution is a small apocalypse of history, judgment within history. . . . Revolution is a sin and the evidence of sin, as war is a sin and the evidence of sin. But revolution is the fate of history, the inevitable destiny of historical existence. In revolution judgment is passed upon the evil forces which have brought about injustice, but the forces which judge, themselves create evil; in revolution good itself is realized by forces of evil, since forces of good were powerless to realize their good in history. And revolutions in Christian history have always been a judgment upon historical Christianity, upon Christians, upon their betrayal of the Christian covenant, upon their distortion of Christianity."[6]

There is always an identifiable sin in the doomed culture—the Caesaro-Papism of the Orthodox Russian Church, which

[6] Nicolas Berdyaev, *The Origin of Russian Communism*, translated by R. M. French, new edition (London, 1948), pp. 131–32.

led to the Revolution, for example. But tragic as the death of a culture may be, Berdyaev exults over the creation of a new spiritual form. Here is the divine manifesting itself again positively and exuberantly in history, as it did in the Middle Ages and Western humanism. Even after punishment has been meted out, a remnant of a great spiritual birth remains forever. The imminent sinking of Europe into another barbaric age is only one movement of history, one apocalypse, and Berdyaev's faith compels him to seek and believe in another spiritualization of man even in the depths of the new darkness in which we are groping.

Thus, with the notable exception of liberal Protestantism, which to all intents and purposes echoes secular progressism, contemporary religious thinkers have all rejected with different degrees of passion the idea of continuous material, cultural, and social progress. For Berdyaev, following his master Vladimir Soloviev, the idea of progress is the seductive teaching of a modern anti-Christ; for Niebuhr, following Karl Barth, a new idolatry; for Dawson, writing in a lower key, a failure to understand the corruption inherent in all things.

III

On a plane only slightly less lofty than the theologians are a group of philosopher-scientists, mostly English and American biologists, whom we might call neo-evolutionists. I said they were chiefly biologists and Anglo-Saxons, although perhaps the most persuasive among them is, after all, the late Jesuit paleontologist Teilhard de Chardin, whose works are now being published posthumously by an international committee. Though throughout his life he was an obedient son of his order and insisted upon the Christological aspects of his doctrine, his writings have been subject to a monitum from the Vatican. He would perhaps have objected to my tearing his ideas out of their "Divine Milieu" (the title of one of his works), but I remain convinced that he more properly belongs among the scientists than the theologians: he is surely closer to Julian Huxley than either to Niebuhr or to Christopher Dawson. What immediately distinguishes this group of evolutionists from the theologians is that while the latter treat of the philosophy of history in terms of eternity, the scientists modestly restrict themselves to billions of years.

These imaginative life-scientists assert that a new spirituality is about to possess mankind and become a permanent acquisition of the species, that we are about to ascend to a higher stage in the autonomous unfolding of the irreversible world-historical process. Physical-biological evolution has virtually reached the utmost limits, they maintain; the development of man, who now has power to control his own evolution, must henceforth take place in the realm of mind or spirit. Teilhard de Chardin wrote of a noösphere, a universal belt of psychosocial forces; Julian Huxley, somewhat less Platonic, prefers the term noösystem. Both of them conceive this to be stage three in the evolution of matter, which has already passed through a historical transformation from the inorganic into the organic, culminating in that unique biological species, man.

If since Cro-Magnon man there has been no perceptible physical evolution of the species, and a Cro-Magnon baby of healthy stock would stand about as good a chance at Stanford University as a Palo Altan, wherein lies the superiority of the Palo Altan? Only in the existence of a transmitted social and psychic order which begins to be absorbed at an early age. The knowledge that sustains this order has accumulated through centuries of time, and future evolutionary progress may be defined as the continuing growth of this vast treasury. The future expanding order of psychosocial inheritances will result in earlier internalization in the child and in ever more complex psychic awareness in the adult. Through the evolving intimacy

and density of the network of human communications throughout the world, a universal morality will be achieved. In the
course of time the process of natural selection will fortify the
new rational and ethical order by showing preference for those
with superior fitness in adapting to it. The old warfare between
nature and culture will be abolished, since both are controlled
by man. The evolutionary process goes on ad infinitum—more
culture in the environment, more natural selection for culture,
and so on until instinctual nature in the raw, the nature that
one body of eighteenth-century thinkers had marked out as the
enemy of culture, is left far behind.

More and more the late Teilhard de Chardin emerges as the
central figure of this twentieth-century cosmic historical myth,
with his arms outstretched to embrace humanist English biologists as well as French Marxists. The vision first came to him
in the mud and slime of the trenches on the Western front during World War I; it persisted through years of exile in China,
where his Order had sent him because of the heterodoxy of his
opinions. His posthumous works have the compelling force of
a voice from the grave calling man to a new life. Teilhard de
Chardin's is a strange historical mysticism in a new language.
He is not bound to the dualism of spirit and matter; materialist is an epithet that no longer frightens him. He sings religious hymns of praise to primeval matter as ultimately creative
of the highest values of spiritual love. At a given moment in
time matter gives birth to consciousness, and consciousness, now
spread over the peoples of the whole planet, by dint of the
sheer physical concentration of a growing population must give
rise to a universal human consciousness—he names the process
hominisation—that will transcend the old individualism.

What Teilhard intoned in a sibylline style, the English and
American biological theorists have been expressing in a plainer
prose, without commitment to Christ and within a purely hu-

manist frame. As Teilhard de Chardin devoted his life to a redefinition of Christology in the light of the new evolutionary vision, so the brilliant English and American biologists have conciliated their new world view with traditional Darwinism by revising its implications. In the nineteenth century Darwin was most commonly—if erroneously—invoked by general historical theorists as an apologist for bloody tooth-and-claw nationalism and imperialism. In the twentieth century, biology has moved away from dramatization of the individual struggle for survival to the idea of evolution by rational choice or direction toward a goal defined in terms not of the virile he-man caricatures of the English eugenicists and the German race theorists of the late nineteenth century but of humane, cooperative, loving, totally conscious beings. These scientists have put a new Darwin by the side of Teilhard de Chardin's new Christ. At one of the darkest moments of the present century Julian Huxley reaffirmed his optimism: "Man represents the culmination of that process of organic evolution which has been proceeding on this planet for over a thousand million years. . . . The appearance of the human type of mind, the latest step in evolutionary progress, has introduced both new methods and new standards. By means of his conscious reason and its chief offspring, science, man has the power of substituting less dilatory, less wasteful, and less cruel methods of effective progressive change than those of natural selection, which alone are available to lower organisms."[7]

Once we are committed to the ideology of cosmic evolution, the narrow five millennia of recorded history with their minor progressions, regressions, cycles, and sinusoidal curves appear terrifyingly diminished. And yet the neo-evolutionists would insist that their teachings are raising man to a higher rather than

[7] Julian S. Huxley, *The Uniqueness of Man* (London, 1941), p. 32.

a lower place in the scheme of things. Far from being dethroned as the king of nature, he is restored to a grander position than he occupied before the Copernician revolution. The earth may now be a mere planet moving around the sun, but man is no longer confined within it. His spiritual energy, his reason, his brain power, his psyche, his consciousness become the center and the purpose of the whole universe, of the cosmic process. The old Adam was ruler of the beasts but subservient to his Creator and on a lower rung than the angels. The new Adam of the humanist biologists, as a result of his own will and struggle, towers in the forefront of all being, the end of billions of years of history—an intoxicating conception, frightening in its hubris, if there are gods to envy him.

The scientists belittle the prophets of doom and dismiss those who are so engrossed in the pettiness of daily living that they fail to see the grand design. In *The Phenomenon of Man,* Teilhard de Chardin places the present in historical perspective: "After all, half a million years, perhaps even a million, were required for life to pass from the pre-hominids to modern man. Should we now start wringing our hands because, less than two centuries after glimpsing a higher state, modern man is still at loggerheads with himself? . . . Planetary movement involves planetary majesty. Would not humanity seem to us altogether static if, behind its history, there were not the endless stretch of its prehistory? Similarly, and despite an almost explosive acceleration of noögenesis at our level, we cannot expect to see the earth transform itself under our eyes in the space of a generation."[8]

From the viewpoint of the scientists ours is an age of crisis not in the sense that two economic systems are at war, or that subject races throughout the world are demanding their share

[8] Pierre Teilhard de Chardin, *The Phenomenon of Man,* translated by Bernard Wall, with an introduction by Julian Huxley (New York, 1959), p. 255.

of goods and their right to participate in universal self-aware-
ness, or that populations and armaments are increasing in un-
precedented numbers: these are conceived merely as the birth
pangs of the new man. It is an age of crisis in the sense that a
new humanity with a sharpened awareness and a deeper consciousness is being forged. Ordinarily this process would be
thought of as requiring millennia in the evolutionary timetable; but some, Teilhard de Chardin among them, are more
sanguine. In the midst of the horrors of the twentieth-century
world they believe that we are actually witnessing the initial
breakthrough. They speak in Nietzschean terms—I hear echoes
of *ein Bruch, ein Zwang*. To these scientists the contemporary
revolution is a leap, not a slow acceleration, and they cite examples from the early history of evolution to justify their conception of discontinuity. In a letter written shortly before his
death, when the nations of the world, East and West, agreed
to cooperate in the scientific investigations of the geophysical
year, Teilhard de Chardin playfully yet enthusiastically proclaimed it the first year of the noösphere.

IV

Another group in the progressist camp are the contemporary
Marxists. It happens that a good number of the English biologists who have participated in the redefinition of Darwinism
are also Marxists, but I really believe that their Marxism is
subordinate to their neo-Darwinian view of evolution. The most
original Marxist school of the twentieth century is by all odds
in France, an important redirection of thought since the nineteenth century, when Marx had only a minimal influence there.
French Marxists of the postwar period rarely burden themselves with the three volumes of *Das Kapital* or Marx's political revolutionary brochures. Like Erich Fromm, they are interested primarily in the young Marx, now dubbed the hu-

manist Marx, the dreamer of freedom from alienation and the prophet of free consciousness for all. The robust Fourierist elements in this Marx of the 'forties are forgotten, and he is remodeled into a genteel, spiritualized, almost clerical figure. Among contemporary French communist intellectuals a new slogan has begun to make its way to the effect that Teilhardism and Marxism are now walking hand in hand into the dawn of a new mankind.[9] The more jaundiced may suspect this entente as another Marxist maneuver, a bold attempt to seize the instruments of salvation, but the engagement seems to be binding enough.

There is also, paradoxically, a sophisticated contemporary French Marxism associated with existentialism that restores Marx to his Hegelian origins and derives intellectual sustenance from his phraseology. Among these Marxists there is a move away from the imagery of the eternal Sabbath in which the golden age of the utopians was bathed. In the twentieth century Nietzsche has been read more deeply by these French intellectuals than by anyone else in the world, and they have felt the sting of his mockery at facile progressist solutions. The dialectical quality of the historical process, the discontinuous character of its movement, a sense of the tragic in history expressed in Hegelian terms transforms this type of French Marxism into a much more subtle doctrine than it ever was when early twentieth-century German revisionists and antirevisionists haggled over the tempo of change and the nature of revolution in purely economic and political terms.

Soviet Marxism is not generally characterized by such French refinements. The shrewd peasant who presided over the destinies of Russia had a meager historical stock-in-trade which consisted of funeral prognostications for others, a few slogans from

---

[9] Roger Garaudy, *Perspectives de l'homme: existentialisme, pensée catholique, marxisme,* 2d edition (Paris, 1960), p. 193.

the Gotha program, and a sentimental conception of the future of art.

But there are other currents of thought in the Soviet Union, not dominant ones to be sure, which draw the conceptions of some Russian thinkers perilously close to those of the progressists and utopian life-scientists of the Western world. Professional historians throughout Eastern Europe leave one with a painful impression of desiccated conservatism: their choice of subjects is often distressingly related to public anniversaries of historical events and threadbare problems of the industrial revolution or of agrarian history, the Russian equivalent of Civil War history in the United States. But more philosophical minds can be found elsewhere than in official historical institutes, and especially among scientists. In May 1961 a colloquium at Royaumont in France brought together a brilliant array of scientists, philosophers, sociologists, and historians, Marxist and non-Marxist, to discuss the subject "What future awaits man?" One of the participants, Nicolai Semenov, member of the Soviet Academy of Sciences and a Nobel Prize winner, took for granted the imminent solution of all economic problems through a vast expansion of nuclear and solar energy, a giant assumption that is common to this type of theory, and then posed the question: What will constitute human activity in the world of tomorrow? His answer could have been that of a Saint-Simonian or an American psychologist with a self-actualization theory. He too echoed the young Marx. "Creative activity, whether it manifests itself through great works or in little things, constitutes at bottom the second essential explicit condition of the genuine happiness of each individual. . . . Today many people see happiness not in creative activity, but, once their work is finished, in giving themselves over to the pleasures of life, tranquil or, at the other extreme, riotous. For my part I am firmly convinced that such a conception of happiness proceeds from spiritual poverty or an emptiness of personality, from the absence of social conditions favoring the expression and development of aspirations and creative capacities that exist potentially in all men."[10]

In this view Semenov was joined by the English Marxist scientist J. D. Bernal, who prophesied a world of endlessly dynamic science rendering life everlastingly exciting with new discovery, a universal republic of scientists that included virtually every man, scientists vying with one another in achievements, which acquire a purely artistic quality since utility becomes superfluous in the midst of bounty. And it is perhaps indicative of a certain community of outlook among the scientists of the world that Semenov's paper was recently reprinted in the American *Bulletin of the Atomic Scientists.*

v

So much for the progressists, spiritual and secular, practical and utopian. The cyclists, with whose antecedents we are by now familiar, are the other major division of contemporary philosophical historians. In Hegelian fashion they tend to avoid the world of prehistory and primitive societies and restrict themselves within the confines of the last five thousand years of civilized history. In their ranks Spengler and Sorokin figure prominently. While polymorphous figures like Toynbee refuse to rest quietly in the Procrustean beds that I have made for them, Toynbee in his first phase is a classical philosopher of the history of what he himself calls the "Age of Civilizations," and he belongs here, even though Toynbee II and Toynbee III may wander off among the theologians and the philosophical evolutionists.

At no time had cyclical theories completely disappeared

---

[10] Rencontre internationale de Royaumont, May 17–20, 1961, *Quel avenir attend l'homme?* (Paris, 1961), pp. 258–59.

from Western culture even though they seemed to be temporarily submerged by late eighteenth- and nineteenth-century theories of progress. The Hegelian sinusoidal system had after all incorporated cyclical elements, as had Saint-Simonism and Marxism. But no pure cyclical doctrine attracted widespread adherence in the nineteenth century. Giuseppe Ferrari's mid-century theory of the repetitive cycle of generations had a limited echo among sociologists. Count Gobineau's adaptation of the cyclical principle to the history of races perhaps produced greater resonance, particularly in Germany. In Brooks Adams America had a cyclical theorist who abused scientific analogies and toyed with *fin de siècle* concepts of decadence. These men were all pygmies, however, by the side of the German philosopher chiefly responsible for the modern revival of the pagan doctrine of eternal recurrence—Friedrich Nietzsche. It was he who denounced the slavishness of a belief in progress that made the last man in the historical series totally dependent upon a long previous array of events and imprisoned him in a unilinear tunnel. Paradoxically, Nietzsche regarded each new phase of a changing circle as an emancipation into novelty and freedom precisely because it was a turning away into a new direction and not a continuation; it was a denial and an overcoming of the past. Since his age had hit rock bottom in putrescence and debility, Nietzsche longed for a new turn of the wheel that would be an affirmation of excellence, virility, and aristocratic yea-saying.

Oswald Spengler's *Decline of the West*, written in its basic draft just prior to World War I, was the formal embodiment of Nietzsche's dithyrambic philosophy in a systematic work. Spengler's value-system was inflamed by a Nietzschean loathing for civilization, for the delusions of progress, and for the rational, all of which were decadent symbols. He idealized the first creative moments of nascent culture, its original mythic and religious forms, its early men of action and will. Spengler blasted the conception of one world-historical continuum—the belief common to Condorcet, Hegel, Marx, and Comte—by setting up a comparison among the life-cycles of eight distinct cultures as if they were air-tight compartments, where nothing, not even a whiff of influence, could penetrate from one to another. Each culture was unique and it experienced an absolutely independent circular history. There were no connexities among cultures, hence no world history.

As the decades go by, Spengler remains the ideal figure of twentieth-century cyclical philosophy of history. For all his hyperbole, false melodrama, dubious fact, he has worn best. Those who came after him opened windows of varying size in the sealed cultural compartments, toned down his language, made it more amenable to Anglo-Saxon sensibility, but the original philosophic imprint is unmistakably his. In a series of four volumes published from 1937 through 1941 the sociologist Pitirim Sorokin added a statistical apparatus and a new terminology. Cultural anthropologists like Alfred Kroeber freed themselves from the rigidity of Spengler's formula for the cultural life span; Ruth Benedict fashioned sensitive psychological typologies for the various cultures; and Toynbee introduced utilitarian explanations for the origins of civilization and a new nomenclature for its successive stages. But in every instance the candid ones who followed Spengler have admitted his spiritual paternity. It was only Spengler with his neo-pagan idea of fated cultural life-cycles who refused to make any compromise with the popular European belief in a unitary universal history moving toward one *telos*. That was for the nursery.

For Spengler, even when there is physical contact and the transmission of writings and works of art, the cultural neighbors cannot understand each other because they speak different psychic languages. While artifacts are communicable, the living spirit is not. When through *force majeure* one culture appears to be diffusing its apperception of the world to another, the result of the meeting is a bastard form, a hothouse-growth doomed to early death. A culture worthy of its name must be lily-pure and cultural miscegenation bears no fruit. As Spengler's horror-piece of what he called a pseudomorphosis stood Russia—a culture that had not yet gone through its appointed seasons of growth when Western Faustian civilization in its last stages was suddenly imposed upon it from without, a crushing burden whose consequence was Bolshevism in 1922, when Spengler published his second volume.

Spengler had no difficulty coping with the doctrine of the progressionists who conceived of world history as a continuous self-transcendence. This was an illusion which sprang from a longing that was unique to the soul of Faustian man, the quest for the infinite in a straight line, an idea that had its counterpart in the cathedral spires of the West, the fugues of its music, and its science.

Toynbee tells us that at one time he was so impressed by Spengler's morphology of civilization that he doubted the need for his own work. But in the end the English writer found it difficult to stomach the Spenglerian absolutism, which demanded that each stage of each culture endure the precise number of years as a parallel stage in every other culture. A gentleman-diplomat of the old school, Toynbee could not make his cultures goosestep before him with split-second timing. And while he recognized the individual personality of civilizations, most of his twenty-one specimens are related to one another through affiliation and apparentation. And the last stages of some civilizations are the chrysalis of the higher religions which, in his most recent volumes, become the real units of history. Totally isolated cultural entities belong only to the first round of civilizations in the ancient world and there have been none for about two thousand years. It is hard for Toynbee to imagine that if there are any future civilizations, they will be divorced from the legacy of existing cultures.

The contrasts between Spengler and Toynbee are profoundly rooted in their respective intellectual heritages. Spengler is dogmatic, Toynbee disarming in his reconsiderations. Spengler collects primarily philosophical, scientific, and aesthetic data, while Toynbee dwells by choice on political, social, and above all religious documents. Toynbee can accept causal historical explanations in a traditional sense; Spengler spurns them since for him the aging process is an inexorable historical-biological rhythm. Perhaps we can discern here the persistence of those two divergent styles of philosophical history that we have dwelt upon before. Toynbee is in the Anglo-French tradition directed outward, a marvelous historical geographer of phenomenal learning who likes to move about the planet. He is in the end a progressist of sorts despite the subsidiary circular curves; if not bursting with optimism he is at least a possibilist about the next age of mankind. Spengler seeks to grasp the inner spirit of cultures. His history is tragic in the Germanic mood, absolutist in its determinism. When a culture passes its heyday and turns into a civilization—an ugly word for him—its death is imminent; and when it dies it leaves no progeny behind. "Civilizations are the most external and artificial states of which a species of developed humanity is capable. They are a conclusion, the thing-become succeeding the thing-becoming, death following life, rigidity following expansion, intellectual age and the stone-built, petrifying world-city following mother-earth and the spiritual childhood of Doric and Gothic. They are an end, irrevocable, yet by inward necessity reached again and again."[11]

---

[11] Oswald Spengler, *The Decline of the West*, translated by C. F. Atkinson (New York, 1926), I, 31.

Sorokin's super-rhythm of alternating sensate-ideational-idealistic cultural super-systems represents the ultimate sophistication of modern cyclical theory; he surpasses all his predecessors in the mass of quantifiable evidence of an arithmetic character that he adduces. Ixion's wheel has become laden with epicycles, with tassels and bells. Though Sorokin resents the slightest intimation that he is a follower of Spengler, when the heart of his system is examined it betrays the same old culture-civilization alternation with a new vocabulary. While he considers the oscillation between ideational and sensate cultures a continuing phenomenon of Western history and sees no sign of a final total collapse or definitive decline of the West, his diagnosis of the civilization of the contemporary world is identical with Spengler's—the adjectives are the same and so is the forbidding inevitability of its end.

If cyclical theory is a myth, with the truth of a myth, the more one lives with these multivolumed twentieth-century versions the more one feels that it may have begun to lose charm. The style has become pompously prophetic, melodramatically emotive, or dismally pedestrian. The *Kyklos* that started out in Empedocles as a poetic contrariety of love and strife has become a monstrous wobbly juggernaut. I can still read Vico and Herder for sustenance, but the twentieth-century overornate, overstuffed, overfootnoted, overgraphed cyclical theories spell for me the end of the cycle of cyclical theories. May I confess it—the cyclical conclusion of Freud's last work, his depiction of the war of Eros and Death, archaistic as it may be, is often more convincing.

VI

Now that we have examined the four groups of philosophical historians, the rather pessimistic theologians, the neo-evolutionists, the neo-Marxists, and the modern cyclists, we may well ask whether there is any measure of agreement among them. At times they diverge so acutely that they seem to be describing different worlds or moving off to the four different cardinal points of the compass.

And yet, much to my amazement, I have found that beneath the surface there is a consensus, albeit an uneasy one, among a substantial body of twentieth-century writers who have examined the historical process in its totality and have ventured to predict its future. They are agreed that the next stage either must or is likely to entail a spiritualization of mankind and a movement away from the present absorption with power and instinctual existence. Toynbee uses the term "etherialisation";[12] in Teilhard de Chardin's private language it is hominisation; the Christian theologians speak in more traditional terms of a recrudescence of religious faith; and Karl Jaspers of a second axial period of spirituality like the age of the prophets, of Buddha, and of Confucius. *Consensus populi* was long ago discarded as a criterion of truth; the consensus of philosophers of history may be an even more dubious witness, but there it stands.

In his most recent writings Toynbee has developed further the image of the ledges on a mountainside which he used in his first volume. One ledge separates the primitive world from the age of civilizations. But this age now is drawing to a close and the rule of circularity which governed the twenty-one specimens of civilized society in the past is not applicable to the future. Civilization, with its inner circular dialectic, is about to be transcended. When man reaches the next ledge, which Toynbee haltingly defines as a spiritual world of brotherhood and communion, new rules will prevail. Toynbee is a hopeful man and not a determinist; catastrophe is forever possible, but it is not likely. As long as man's response surpasses the challenge, creative life will continue on a higher level. The cycles of civili-

---

[12] Arnold Toynbee, *A Study of History*, XII (London, 1961), 267.

zation have been merely turns in the wheel of the divine chariot. From the vantage point of a tortured man bound to the wheel like Ixion, this was perhaps a meaningless set of revolutions; but there was always the driver and he had the prospect of moving toward a more human and a more spiritual destiny. Even the circular philosophers of history or cultural sociologists who hold fast to an iron law of the circle from which there is no release, men like Spengler and Sorokin, nevertheless testify that the next period will see a rebirth of spirit. The contemporary civilization of gigantism, sensation, and technics has exhausted its creative capabilities and a new ideational, mystical, or religious form is about to be born somewhere. The organization of megalopolis under the direction of the engineer, the key figure of the final stage of Western Faustian culture, may continue for awhile, writes Spengler in the last pages of his second volume, but have no illusions. One fine day the engineer in quest of his soul's salvation, heeding the claims of his inner being, will abandon the machines and the technological civilization will collapse. What will replace it? First a "fellahin idiocy," and then a new mythology expressive of a new spiritual existence which Spengler refuses to define because no one can describe the face of the unborn. In 1941 Sorokin assured his audience at the Lowell Institute in Boston that they had the privilege of living in the crisis period of one of those rare phenomena, a revolution from a sensate to an ideational culture. Even the Christian philosophers of history who, in their anxiety to stress the truth of the Augustinian drama, are reluctant to bestow great meaning upon secular history, have nonetheless joined the chorus of those who believe that the present historical moment is exposing the utter falsity of Condorcet's heresy of infinite earthly progress and that a religious revival, if not inevitable, is at least probable.

Thus there emerges a most unexpected consensus among re-

ligious thinkers and Marxists gone spiritual, the English humanist biologists and the Jesuit mystic, Cassandras of the fall
of the West and Greek Orthodox visionaries. The union is a
paradoxical one, but the twentieth century has offered us so
many bizarre political alignments that these strange intellectual bedfellows should not really shock us.

There is of course an important cleavage among them: those
who define the new spirituality as one more act in a series,
either part of a slow continuing process or another leap into a
higher state of consciousness, and those for whom the coming
age of the spirit is merely an episode of cyclical renewal after
a period of total disintegration. You are thus left with the
choice of spirituality leading to a transfiguration of our materialist civilization, or spirituality born after its apocalyptic breakdown. But in either event, the reign of the spirit is upon us.

To be sure, there is an important holdout against this new
spiritual vision, the old-fashioned rationalistic sensationalist
progressists and meliorists of the Anglo-French tradition, and
they probably comprise the vast majority of human beings in
the world today. For them the civilization that so colorfully
passes in review as one drives along the Champs Elysées, Fifth
Avenue, the Via Veneto, and El Camino Real can endure forever, constantly becoming more luminous until night turns into
day. But few of the contemporary philosophers of history seem
to believe in its continuance.

As a member of the generation of 1910 I have seen my fill
of horror in war and peace. I am no Pangloss, nor Professor
Tout-va-bienovitch, that Russian doctor fashioned by Céline's
mordant wit. In the midst of universal dread of nuclear annihilation, world-wide social revolution, internecine racial wars,
the spectacle of fat-land inhabitants committing suicide by over-
feeding and of barren lands incapable of preventing the mass

starvation of their hungry, the assurances of the prophets of the new spirituality often seem utopian, even a hollow joke. The victims of the twentieth-century slaughterhouse refuse to believe it.

As a skeptic I am reluctant to receive the witness of the heralds of the new spirit, and yet it is pouring in upon me from so many diverse sources and directions that I am on the point of surrendering my belief in the ordinary evidence of the senses. I stand on the verge of accepting the new dispensation. But in what version? Is this triumph of spirit a stage in an infinite progress up Jacob's ladder or is it merely another turn of Ixion's wheel? Here doubt assails me without a remedy, and I take refuge in Master David Hume's conclusion to the *Natural History of Religion* when he was confronted by a similar dilemma:

"The whole is a riddle, an ænigma, an inexplicable mystery. Doubt, uncertainty, suspence of judgment appear the only result of our most accurate scrutiny, concerning this subject. But such is the frailty of human reason, and such the irresistible contagion of opinion, that even this deliberate doubt could scarcely be upheld; did we not enlarge our view, and opposing one species of superstition to another, set them a quarrelling; while we ourselves, during their fury and contention, happily make our escape into the calm, though obscure, regions of philosophy."[13]

[13] David Hume, *The Natural History of Religion*, edited with an introduction by H. E. Root (Stanford, 1957), p. 76.

Index

Index